Washington Gladden

The Lord's Prayer

Seven Homilies

Washington Gladden

The Lord's Prayer
Seven Homilies

ISBN/EAN: 9783743336735

Manufactured in Europe, USA, Canada, Australia, Japa

Cover: Foto ©ninafisch / pixelio.de

Manufactured and distributed by brebook publishing software (www.brebook.com)

Washington Gladden

The Lord's Prayer

CONTENTS.

		PAG.
PREFACE	. . . .	5
I. THE ETERNAL FATHER	. . . . .	9
II. THE SACRED NAME	. . . . . .	34
III. THE ETERNAL KINGDOM	. . . .	59
IV. THE BLESSED WILL	. . . . .	82
V. THE CONVENIENT FOOD	. . . .	106
VI. THE FORGIVING GRACE	. . . . .	129
VII. THE GREAT SALVATION	. . . .	167

PREFACE.

THE provocation of these homilies was a series of short but incisive letters, written by Mr. John Ruskin to an English clergyman, but published by the writer's consent in the "Contemporary Review," and meant for all the English clergy. I quote some of his questions.

"Can this Gospel of Christ be put into such plain words and short terms that a plain man can understand it? and if so, would it not be, in a quite primal sense, desirable that it should be so?"

And again:—

"I want only to put this sterner question to your council, how this Gospel is to be preached 'everywhere' or 'to all nations,' if first its preachers have not determined quite clearly what it is. And might not such definition, acceptable to the entire body of the Church of Christ, be arrived at by merely explaining in their completeness and life the terms of the Lord's Prayer — the first words taught to children all over the Christian world?"

And again: —

"My meaning in saying that the Lord's Prayer might be made a foundation of Gospel-teaching was not that it contained all that Christian ministers have to teach; but that it contains what all Christians are agreed upon as first to be taught; and that no good parish-working pastor in any part of the world but would be glad to take his part in making it clear and living to his congregation."

Though I am not a member of the communion for which these letters of Mr. Ruskin were intended, I could not help feeling the force of his suggestions, and this small volume is one fruit of them. Whatever value the reader may discover in these studies, the writer has gained by means of them not only a better understanding of the Lord's Prayer, but an altogether new sense of the wideness of its range and the fullness of its meaning.

NORTH CHURCH STUDY *Springfield, Mass.*

THE LORD'S PRAYER.

I.

THE ETERNAL FATHER.

Our Father who art in heaven. — MATT. vi. 9.

It is an old path to whose entrance we turn our faces when we begin to study the Lord's Prayer, — an old path and well-worn by the feet of many incurious worshipers and many devout interpreters. What then? Are there no ways worth walking in but those uncertain trails blazed for us by pioneers through tangled forests on the frontiers of faith? Old roads there are that offer fair prospects and that lead to pleasant places; where the hedgerows every year are sweet with blossoms and musical with birds; from beneath whose sheltering rocks the living water springs as cool and fresh to-day as when our fathers drank thereof.

The prayer that Christ taught his disciples is not a threadbare formula; it is as full as it ever was of fresh and vital truth. And while we dwell upon its familiar phrases, let us trust that his own Spirit, which takes of the things that he has left and makes them plain to us, will abide with us, helping us now to understand, and evermore devoutly and trustfully to use, the petitions that are grouped in this simple form of words.

The first thing to be noted is the brevity of this prayer. This is especially significant when taken in connection with the words which the Saviour had just been speaking. "When ye pray use not vain repetitions as the heathen do, for they think that they shall be heard for their much speaking Be ye not therefore like unto them." In most of the other religions the efficacy of prayer has been supposed to depend on its length. The notion is that the gods will do nothing for men unless they are teased. And even the Jews themselves had fallen into this error, for our Lord denounces the Pharisees who devour widows' houses, and for a pretense (or for a mask of their wickedness) make long prayers. We know that long prayers are quite the fashion now among devout Jews; one of the maxims of the Rabbis is, "Prolix prayer protracts life." At the sacrament of circumcision the prescribed prayers of orthodox Jews are repeated with great rapidity, for the reason that if they were deliberately read a whole day would be consumed in reading them.

It was not the Gentiles alone, then, but his own people as well, that Jesus was rebuking by his warning against vain repetitions and long prayers. This prayer that he has left us is so short that one who utters it very slowly will finish it within one minute. And while many times we cannot tell our Father in heaven within the space of one minute all the things that we want to tell him, — while we cannot always relieve our own burdened spirits without a longer season of communion with him than that, — yet it is true beyond a doubt that we often err as the Jews and the Gentiles did in supposing that we are heard for our much speaking. No doubt many of our public prayers, especially in pulpit and prayer-meeting, would be far more effectual if they followed more nearly the pattern set for us in the brevity of the Lord's Prayer.

Two or three more questions ought to be answered before we proceed with our study.

How was this prayer to be used? Was it to be used exclusively? So some persons have supposed. In Luke's version of the prayer he reports the Master as prefacing it with the words, " When ye pray, say, Our Father who art in heaven," etc. Therefore it has been inferred that he meant to give them a form of words which they were always to use, and that they were never to use any other words of prayer. But it is plain that this cannot be his meaning, because we have a record in the Acts of the Apostles of several prayers which did not follow this form of words, and which were answered abundantly. To confine his disciples to a single form of prayer would have been exactly contrary to the whole spirit of his teaching.

But if we are at liberty to use other words when we pray, ought we always when we pray to use these words — to *include* this prayer in all our supplications? No; I do not think that our Lord means to require that. We shall often wish to pray in these words; but he means that our desires shall be free to utter themselves in their own way. In Matthew's report of the prayer, our Lord begins by saying: "*After this manner*, therefore, pray ye." The prayer is a model, in its simplicity, its brevity, its directness; but it is not a prescribed form; it is a staff and not a fetter for the praying soul.

Was it the design of the Master that this prayer, or indeed that any prayer, should be used publicly? Some things that are said in this Sermon on the Mount would seem to answer this question in the negative. "When thou prayest thou shalt not be as the hypocrites are; for they love to pray standing in the synagogues and in the corners of the streets, that they may be seen of men. Verily I say unto you, they have their reward. But thou, when thou prayest, enter into thy closet, and when thou hast shut thy door, pray to thy Father which is in secret; and thy Father which seeth in secret shall reward thee openly." Does this forbid all public prayer? Certainly it does if we are always to take the Bible just as it reads — to interpret all its sayings literally. No command could be more express than this of our Lord, not to pray in the synagogues, but when we pray to enter into the closet and shut the door. Yet we know that our Lord himself sometimes prayed in the presence of others. He prayed at the tomb of Lazarus; he prayed in the upper room with his disciples on the night of the Last Supper — that prayer of triumphant faith and deathless love which John has recorded in the seventeenth chapter of his Gospel. We know, too, that the prayers of his disciples, when they were all with one accord in one place, and there lifted up their supplications, were richly answered. So, then, we infer that this preface of the Lord's Prayer is not to be taken literally; that it is only a strong rebuke of ostentatious praying, — of the hypocrisy which prays to be heard and seen of men. Indeed, all true prayer in public is a kind of secret prayer; for, though the one who prays stands or kneels among his fellow-men, he is as much alone with God as if he were in his closet. He may think of those who listen; he may seek to put himself in their places and to be the voice of their desires and their confessions; but the moment he begins to think of what they are thinking about his prayer, that moment he ceases to pray. Prayer in the assembly, as well as in the solitude, is "the flight of one alone to the only One."

Let us turn now to the first sentence of the Lord's Prayer, which shall be our theme for a little while this morning.

Our Father who art in heaven. Did the people to whom this Sermon on the Mount was spoken know before this that God was their Father? It is confessed that they had clearer ideas about God than any other people in the world; was this thought that he is our Father among their common thoughts of him?

No, it was not. I believe that the word Father is applied to God seven times in the Old Testament; among the innumerable references to the Supreme Being which crowd almost every chapter of all the books of the Old Testament but one, he is mentioned just seven times as a Father, — five times as the Father of the Hebrew people, twice as sustaining that relation to individuals. Of these two intimations that God is the Father of individual men, one is a promise to David that God will be a father to his son, Solomon; the other is a prediction that by and by men will pray to God calling him Father,—a prediction fulfilled in this prayer. For there is no record of any *prayer* in the Old Testament in which God is addressed as Father. We have the words of several prayers in which the holy men of God called upon him by the names that they best knew him by, but there is not one in which they address him as their Father. "In the vocative case, as an address to God in prayer," says Dean Mansel, the name of Father "does not occur in the Old Testament."

It was, then, practically a new thought about God which our Saviour gave his disciples when he taught them about God. They had always known him as the Eternal, the Creator, the Self-existent One, the Supreme Ruler, the Judge, the Lord of Hosts or of Battles, the Captain of the armies of heaven; but this thought of him as the Father in heaven was one that was very far from all their common thoughts of him. When a prayer was given them in which this name, and this name only, was applied to him, — when they were taught to think of him as their Father, and to come to him with the freedom and the confidence that a little child feels in coming to its father, it is certain that a wonderful change must have taken place in all their religious ideas and feelings. This word took them into a new world. I do not think that any of us can begin to imagine the revolution that was made in the religious life of the disciples of Christ when they began to say, "Our Father in Heaven," and began, though dimly, to understand that in all its tender and winning suggestions the word was not only true, but that it was far within the truth. It was to them as if they had been standing for a long time before the grim outer walls of some old castle which they had been summoned to enter, — stand ing there and looking doubtfully at the forbidding granite battlements, with cannon and sentries on the ramparts, with suggestions of gloomy passages and dungeons and chains within, — when all at once a little door opened, and they saw within the wall a pleasant garden, with flowers and fountains and cool retreats, and caught a breath of the sweetest odors, and heard a burst of melody from singing birds and happy children playing in the sun. Such an opening into the very heart of God did this word Father make for all who had stood for long in the cold shadow of the old monarchical conception of his character. There was meaning in the word of the Master when he said, "I am the Door."

One thing, however, these disciples did not need to learn about God, and that was his personality. If they had not known that God was a Person, this word would have taught it to them; but they did know it. Whatever else their special training had failed to do for the Jews, it had not failed to convey to them the truth that God is a conscious Person; that he has intelligence in some respects like ours, yet infinitely transcending ours; that he has affection, and free will, so that he can love his children and choose their welfare. Mr. Matthew Arnold tries to make out that the earlier Hebrews did not believe in a personal Deity (which is a monstrous inversion of the facts of the Biblical history), but even he asserts that in the later days of the nation this belief was universal among them.

The word Father did not help them in forming the idea of the Divine Personality; they had believed God to be a Person; only it was, as we have said, a different kind of person that they had thought of when they had thought of him, — it was a King, or a Judge, or a Warrior, and not a loving Father.

To us, however, this word may be precious, not so much in giving us the idea of the personality of God, as in helping us to hold on to it. For although this doctrine may be abused, and often is; though men who speak of God as a Person often mean by that that he is altogether such an one as themselves, thus degrading his character and limiting his power; nevertheless it is essential to all true worship and to all fruitful religious thought that we keep hold of this idea, — that he is something more than a law or a system of laws, something better than a force or a universe of forces, something diviner than the order of nature or "the stream of tendency by which all things fulfill the laws of their being," — that he is a conscious Person, a living, loving Father.

Just at this time there is special need of reaffirming this truth. For the study of physical science, which is simply a study of the laws of physical nature, has come to occupy so large a place in the interest of men that many of them have been inclined to insist upon the hasty and foolish conclusion that there is no God but nature and its forces, that the All is God, and that there is no other. This is Pantheism — and there are many forms of it. Some Pantheists seem to think that God is simply the sum of all things that are; others teach, with Spinoza, that God is the universal substance — the substance out of which all the worlds and all their works were made; (who made them I wonder?) others that the forces which act and react in nature, — gravitation, cohesion, chemical affinity, heat, light, electricity and the rest, — that these are God; others say, with Fichte, that God is the universal moral order. But all these theories agree in this, that they identify God with the universe; they strip him of all individuality; they make of him only an immense aggregation of things or a group of forces or a principle of morality or something else abstract or impersonal.

I will not stop to show how unphilosophical this notion is, though that is not a hard thing to do; I only wish to point out that this word, by which our Lord teaches us to pray to his and our Father, is the very antithesis of Pantheism. It affirms exactly what Pantheism denies. If God is our Father he is surely a conscious Person. No Pantheist can use the words of the Lord's Prayer in their obvious and natural meaning. None of them except Renan, I think, has ever attempted it. He seems to belong to a class of Pantheists whose views are concisely expressed by Eckhart, one of the old mystics: "God is nothing and God is something; that which is something is also nothing; what God is he is altogether." I should like to see anybody go to work to disprove that statement. Hegel also appears to take the same view. He says that "pure being is pure nothing," which comes near to being pure nonsense. Renan belongs to this school, apparently, and in a book which he wrote a good while ago he made use of this expression, "Our Father, the Abyss!" Our Father, the Abyss! Orphaned indeed must he be who can find neither in the universe nor above it any Father but an abyss, bottomless, boundless, sightless, thoughtless.

Now right over against these mystical absurdities, this system which confounds God and nature, is the blessed truth of the text told in this word Father, — one word that is worth as much more than all the scholastic arguments of Pantheism as bread is worth more than stones to a hungry man.

O you who are tired out with the work and the battle of this laborious life, and are longing for rest and home and love; you who are saddened by losses and bereavements here, and are pining for consolation and sympathy that men cannot give you; you who have found that sin is too strong for you, and are crying out for help to overcome it, — are you satisfied when men point you to the forces of nature or the laws of the moral universe, or worse than all, to an abyss of non-existence, and tell you to find there the help that you are looking for? This is all that Pantheism has to offer you. Is it enough? It is like offering to a man who is famishing with thirst a Report of the Water Commissioners of some foreign city, printed in an unknown tongue.

I have only time left to touch in the most hasty and superficial way half a dozen inferences from this short phrase, each of which demands a full hour for its adequate consideration.

And first, the truth contained in this new name of God is the true constructive idea in all theological science. Build all your theologies on this foundation. Hold fast to the idea of uniform law, of a nature of things which God has established, under which sin is punished; but when you speak of the personal character and government of God, of his direct interference in the affairs of men, of what he does supernaturally, in the order of history, remember that he is our Father. The theologies of the past have been built mainly upon the monarchical rather than the paternal idea of God. In their *religious life*, all Christians have kept hold of the truth that God is their Father; in their *theological speculations* they have chosen rather to emphasize the representation that he is a Moral Governor; and all their reasonings about his administration have been based upon this idea; all their statements and inferences of what he can do and cannot do, what he must do and must not do, have been drawn from the analogies of human governments; from the rules of policy and expediency that human rulers have found it necessary for them to adopt. This is a very unsafe method of reasoning. The highest conception of God that the Bible gives us is the one that should rule in all our theological speculations, and that is the conception which Christ gives us in the word Father.

The word suggests to us also the dignity of human nature. It is a reaffirmation of that primal truth that we find in the first book of the Bible, that man is made in the image and likeness of God. " Behold what manner of love the Father has bestowed upon us that we should be called the sons of God." He who was before all worlds, he whose will is the source of all laws, he who is the life of all that live, the Omnipotent, the Allwise, the Eternal God, is our Father.

"*Our* Father." The word not only lifts up and glorifies every humblest human creature, it binds together in one brotherhood, in one family, all that dwell upon the face of the earth. It is the grand leveler of ranks and hierarchies; it is the charter of fraternity; it is the prophecy of peace and good-will among men. When you say "Our Father," whom do you include in that word "our?" Nay, whom do you dare to exclude? It sweeps us all in; it gathers into one waiting company the king and the beggar, the philosopher and the hind, the Hellene and the Hottentot, the saint and the sinner; it confesses the parentage and the dignity and the worth of every human soul, and cries, in the simple words of Tiny Tim, " God bless us every one." What a prayer this is that reaches up so high and down so low and forth so far; the breadth and length and depth and height of whose simplest petitions we often so feebly utter!

Again, what help and inspiration there is for us in the thought of the relationship here pointed out! Take it home to yourself, my brother. Try to make out something of what it means when you say that God is your Father. Doubtless it means a great deal. Doubtless there is more of comfort and strength in it than you have ever got out of it.

Mayhap you are despised and trodden under foot of men, having almost lost your self-respect. Lift yourself up; let no man despise you! God is your Father! You are the heir of his love; you ought to be a sharer in his glory.

You may be in poverty and wretchedness; hunger is pinching you and toil is wearing you out; but do not lose heart God is your Father; do not doubt that you are just as dear to him as those are who have more of this world's goods than you, and that the time will come when they as well as you will see that it is so. Never give way to repining; never suffer yourself to fall into that state of shamefacedness and abjectness in which so many of the poor are found; never accept the world's false estimates of worth. If other men seem to think that because you are poor you are therefore of little account, do not *you* believe it. Remember that God is your Father. Respect yourself for your Father's sake.

It may be that you are lamenting the passing of those who were very dear, and that your path lies through a shadow of darkness that can be felt; forget not in your sorrow that "like as a father pitieth his children so the Lord pitieth them that fear him." He loves you far more tenderly than you loved those that are gone; he would not have taken them from you but for wise and good reasons.

It may be that you have slipped and sunk into the mire of some great wickedness but though men may have turned their backs on you God has not forsaken you. If there is in your heart the faintest desire to be reclaimed from your iniquities, he knows it and delights to see it; he will not leave you to perish in your degradation, but will lift you up and succor you if you will only let him.

Whoever you are, whatever your needs and your griefs may be, whatever your sins may have been, this truth, that God is your Father, ought to be to you a truth full of encouragement and inspiration.

"The new charity," as one of its wisest apostles said in Boston the other day, "seeks to provide every needy family with a friend." If we could only make every needy family — those needy ones that live in the palaces, as well as those that live in the cellars — see that they have one Friend already, could make him known to them, could get them to trust in him, what a blessed light would shine into many desolate homes!

Here is a young man just setting out in life. He has his own way to make, and he finds that the currents of human selfishness and greed are sometimes hard to stem. He sees that others about him have influential friends who often help them over hard places, and he says to himself sometimes: "I wish I had a friend, some one with experience and influence, to whom I could go now and then; not that I want material aid, but I would like to know some wise and strong man who would believe in me, and be glad when I went right, and say so; and give me moral rather than financial backing in my endeavor to do an honorable and successful business." Such a friend a young business man sometimes finds, and such a friendship is often invaluable.

This is only an allegory by which the inner history of every human soul is visibly set forth. Every one who seeks the true riches finds the needs of a friend whose counsel he may trust, on whose strength he may lean. You have such a Friend, my brother; one whose wisdom is infinite and whose resources are unfailing; one who believes in you, who never loses his hold on any human soul so long as there is a spark of good left in it; one who is glad when you do well, and wants to do nothing so much as to help you to do better; one who stoops to lift you up when you fall, and to lead you out of the ways of peril into the ways of safety; one in whose presence ten thousand mighty angels, who look always on his face and behold its joy, strike their golden harps with sympathetic gladness whenever one sinner forsakes his sin.

"Our Father *in heaven!*" Where it is I know not; what it is no man fully knows. But it is where Our Father is. And whoever is with him is not far from heaven. Something of the melody of its music, something of the fragrance and the beauty of its sweet fields, steal into his heart even while he walks along the dusty ways of this lower world. Do you fancy that there was much difference with Enoch, say, between the before and the after? God took him — *how* I do not know; but though it may be a little less grand, it is no less sweet to walk with God along the humble paths of daily duty than to ride forth with him so royally " on cherub and on cherubim." The track of that chariot I will not try to trace; I only care to know that if I am changed into his image through faith in him, I shall awake in his likeness and be satisfied.

II.

THE SACRED NAME.

Hallowed be thy name. — MATT. vi. 9.

THE fact that great things have small beginnings is as true in morals as it is in biology. The deepest and most universal moral sentiments show traces of a humble origin. The love of moral purity was nourished by habits of physical purity. Cleanliness is next to godliness, — next before it, indeed, in the order of time. The washings and purifications of the Jews were a ritual drill, out of which the sentiment of moral purity was developed.

Likewise, the great sentiment of reverence was planted in a sterile and unfriendly soil, and kept alive by many merely formal observances. To imagine that men in the earliest ages had the same kind of reverence for God that good men have in the present day would be a great error. They were afraid of the various manifestations of force that they saw in nature; but of genuine reverence they knew but little. Here and there a religious genius, like Abraham or Melchisedek, gained some insight into divine things; but the great majority had but a dim apprehension of the real character of God, and could not therefore have felt any true reverence for him. It was possible, however, for these ignorant and unspiritual people to be trained in certain outward observances which would lead them toward reverence. To this end they were instructed to hold the name Jehovah in scrupulous regard. It was not freely spoken; even in reading the Scriptures it was passed over in silence; some other name of God less sacred was substituted for it. After a time the true pronunciation of this name was lost by the Jewish people themselves, and it has never been regained. It passed from the lips of the people; the sound of it was forgotten; and scholars who have studied the documents and the monuments of antiquity are at a loss to determine what the original pronunciation was. Probably, however, it was more nearly like Yahveh than like Jehovah.

The result of what seems to us the superstitious treatment of a name was, however, the deepening in the hearts of the people of the sentiment of reverence. In having it so firmly impressed upon their minds that the name of God must not be lightly used, they were also made to feel that the Person and character of God ought to be honored. The name stood for the Person. The Person they could not see; but if they were taught to be silent in the presence of his name, they would learn that his being, as well as the word that represented it to them, was holy.

The third commandment undoubtedly includes this thought, though I doubt if it is the principal thought. It is against perjury rather than profanity that the commandment is chiefly directed. "Thou shalt not swear falsely in the name of the Lord" is the primary meaning. But the wrongfulness of appealing to God's name lightly and wantonly is also suggested; and there are many other passages in the Levitical Law where this sin is clearly forbidden and threatened with condign punishment.

Under this training there sprung up in the minds of devout Jews a certain reverence for the sacred name, which, under more spiritual teaching, should grow into reverence for the divine character. And this teaching our Lord is now supplying.

What name is this that He is teaching us to hallow in our prayers? God had been known thus far by many names. He was first revealed as Elohim, the God of nature, the Creator, — a name to which in the early Scriptures no moral attributes are attached. He was known also to the early patriarchs as El-Schaddai — the God Almighty. He was known also as the Holy One of Israel, — and as the Lord of Hosts. Above all, He declared himself by that name of which we have been speaking, which in our version is rendered Jehovah, — or for which the word LORD in small capitals is substituted, — which seems to mean the Self-existent and Eternal Being. And now Jesus teaches us to address him as our Father. Which of these names are we here bidden to hallow?

As soon as we ask this question it at once becomes plain that "name" is not used here in the narrow verbal sense of which we have been speaking, but in a wider and larger sense. It is not merely the letters and syllables that spell the name by which God is known that our Lord teaches us here to sanctify. The petition includes, I suppose, all the names by which God has revealed himself. As the God of Nature, as the Lord Almighty, as the Lord of Sabbaoth, as the Holy One of Israel, as the Eternal and Self-existent One, as the Heavenly Father, in all the characters that he bears, he is to be reverenced and glorified.

There is no word that is large enough to hold all the truth that God has told men about himself. He must needs choose many different words under which to declare to men different attributes and phases of his own character. And when all these words are uttered the half is not told.

> "Join all the glorious names
> Of wisdom, love, and power
> That mortals ever knew,
> That angels ever bore;
> All are too mean to speak his worth,
> Too mean to set his glories forth!"

And it is not only by words that he has made himself known. In the order and the beauty of the universe he discloses himself, signs of his presence and proofs of his power are shown us in the things that he has made that no words could ever have given us.

> "The Lord our God is Lord of all,
> His station who can find?
> I hear him in the waterfall,
> I hear him in the wind.

> "If in the gloom of night I shroud,
> His face I cannot fly;

I see him in the evening cloud
And in the morning sky."

And not only in the words of the Book and the laws and lives of the world does he display himself to discerning minds, but also in the movements of the race; in the slowly unfolding plans of his loving providence; in the increasing purpose that runs through the ages. And he who stands with reverent spirit in the track of the world's progress, and who knows enough of the past to have any sense of historical perspective, may well cry out: —

"O God, our God, thou shinest here,
Thine own this latter day;
To us thy radiant steps appear;
Here beams thy glorious ray.

"The fathers had not all of thee;
New births are in thy grace;
All open to our souls shall be
Thy glory's hiding-place.

"Thou comest near; thou standest by;
Our work begins to shine:
Thou dwellest with us mightily;
On speed the years divine!"

And not only in the names by which the Bible describes him, and in the forms in which the creation reveals him, and in the events by which history unveils his presence, but also in the person of him who was the brightness of his glory and the express image of his person, who is the Word, that reveals God to men; who could say of himself, "He that hath seen me hath seen the Father," is God made known to men.

> "Son of the Father! Lord most high!
> How glad is he who finds thee nigh!
> Come in thy hidden majesty;
> Fill us with love, fill us with thee."

And not only in the written word, and in the created universe, and in the broadening stream of progress, and in the person of his Son, but also in the heart of the humble and contrite believer, does God reveal himself.

> "Oh not in circling depth or height,
> But in the conscious breast, —
> Present to faith though veiled from sight,
> There doth his spirit rest;
> Oh come thou Presence infinite
> And make thy creatures blest."

And these are only parts of the ways in which the Infinite One unveils his glories to the thought of his children. Indeed we may say that the whole of creation, the whole of providence, the whole of history, is simply God's method of revealing himself. The things that are, the forces that work, the events that take place, are only manifestations of the power and wisdom and love of the infinite God. Because of the perverseness of human wills and the corruption of human natures this manifestation is often imperfect; we see as through a glass, darkly; but the dimness is not in the light that shines, it is in the medium through which it shines; these refracted and broken rays disclose to us all that we are able to receive of the glory and beauty of the Eternal God our Father.

Now the name of God includes all by which he is or may be known to us. It is not only in the sub-vocal consonants of the Hebrew tongue that it is spelled; in the shining alphabet of crystals and the rude forms of fossils the geologist writes it for us; with pencil of starlight the astronomer inscribes it upon the sky; the flowers are a bright anthology that preserve for us part of its secret; the fall and the rising again of empires and dynasties are the solemn articulations by which its majesty is syllabled; the character of the Son of Man is a perfect utterance of it in the language of the human life, and the Comforter who comes in his name translates that for us into the terms of everyday experience.

Now as I understand this first petition it includes the thought that all these distinct but conspiring revelations of God are to be reverenced. Whatever helps us to a fuller knowledge of him — his nature, his character, his purposes, his works — ought to be held sacred. All these forms of truth, all these methods of disclosure by which he is seeking to make himself known, should be reverently treated. It is not only that part of his name which is given to us in the

Bible, but every other part of his name that we have learned, or that he has sought to communicate to us, that we ought to hallow. And the men who contemn or even ignore the truths of science or the facts of history or the witness of the Christian consciousness cannot offer this prayer without judging themselves.

"Whoever is afraid of science," says the Rev. Newman Smyth, "does not believe in God. Though the truths which the several sciences have discovered in the various fields of inquiry are with difficulty brought together and harmonized; though the facts of nature, history, and consciousness lie before our reason, often uncovered and broken, like those fragments of Assyrian records which have been thrown together in the British Museum; we should, nevertheless, regard every one of them as of value, and as having its own place and worth in the record of God's creative purpose, which, some day, we may hope not merely to decipher in syllables and to know in part, but to comprehend in its length and its breadth, and to read as one grand connected story."[1]

But the name of God stands for God himself, and I suppose that when we intelligently offer this prayer we express the desire not only that the various revelations which God has made to men may be reverently treated, but that God himself may be honored in our thoughts and in our conduct.

To hallow is either to make holy or to consider and recognize as holy. We cannot by our words nor by our deeds add any essential holiness to the Holy One of Israel; but we can think holy thoughts about him; we can sanctify him in our hearts.

We all believe that there is only one God in heaven; but there is another sense in which it is true that every man worships a God of his own, unlike the God in heaven, unlike the deities worshiped by his fellows. For no man's conception of

---

[1] *Old Faiths in New Light*, p. 24.

God is perfect; and the character which each man ascribes to God is blurred by his own ignorance and distorted by his own imagination. There is only one President Hayes in Washington; but the President Hayes whom you think of when I speak his name may be a very different man from the one I think of, and both may be very different from the reality. If each one of the citizens of the United States could give an accurate mental photograph of the President, as he conceives his character, we should have a great variety of pictures.

Now the conceptions of the character of God that men entertain differ far more than their conceptions of the character of their fellow-men, because the range of thought is wider; elements of mystery enter in that do not enter into men's estimates of their neighbors; and while every representation that men can make to themselves of the Infinite Father must be imperfect and unworthy of him, yet some are far more imperfect than others. And in this petition we are taught to ask that our thoughts of God may be freed from error and cleansed from corruption; that our conception of his character may be corrected and enlarged and hallowed, so that it shall come nearer to the ineffable divine reality.

Every man's religion, every man's character, will greatly depend upon his thought of God. If God is to him a tyrant, the mere incarnation of will, whose justice is the simple impulse to destroy all creatures that transgress his law, then the man's religion must needs be a slavish worship and a groveling fear. If, on the other hand, God is to him a good-natured and weakly indulgent Father, who does not care much whether his children do right or wrong, and who expends the resources of his omnipotence in preserving them from the destruction which they court by their misdeeds, the religion of this man will be apt to be simple recklessness; he will stifle Paul's indignant scruple, and continue in sin that grace may abound. And whatever defect we ascribe to God in our thought, not only our theologies but our lives are likely to be perverted by it. It is therefore of the very first importance that our thought of God should be a large and pure and worthy thought; that we do not belittle and dishonor him by our imaginations. And by no petition that we can utter can we express a deeper need of our lives than we do by this petition that God may be hallowed in our thoughts.

But how shall we who are unholy think holy thoughts of God? Must not the thought be as the thinker? How can a pure stream issue from an impure source? Is it possible for us, by any energy of our own, to correct the aberrations of our mental vision and replace the distorted images of God that fill our minds with those that more perfectly represent him? Certainly not; and, therefore, this is a prayer for divine illumination and cleansing; for the gift of that Spirit which searcheth all things, yea, the deep things of God, and reveals them unto men. It is a prayer that God himself will come to us, and abide in our thoughts, and make himself known to us in all his glorious holiness.

But the name of the Lord is hallowed, not only by treating with reverence the revelations that he has made of himself, and by thinking pure and worthy thoughts about him, but also by adding, as we can, to the respect and honor in which his name is held among men. God as well as men has a name — that is to say, a reputation — in the earth. He is held by all his children in a certain estimation. And it is of great consequence that this name that he bears be an honorable and illustrious name; that what men call his declarative glory be promoted. It is not only important that you and I think worthy thoughts about him, it is important also that we do all we can to increase the honor in which he is held.

Every dutiful child wishes his father to be honored by all who know him. The testimonies of others to his father's worth fill him with thankfulness; any injury that threatens his father's reputation causes him pain. And so the true child of God desires that all men should love and revere his Father in heaven; that not only the goodly fellowship of the prophets, and the noble army of martyrs, and the glorious company of the apostles, with cherubim and seraphim should praise him, but that all men everywhere should honor him; that earth as well as heaven should be filled with the majesty of his glory. So when we pray that his name may be hallowed, this is part of what we pray for, — that not only in our own thoughts but in the thoughts of all men he may be honored; that not only by our own lips but by the lips of all to whom he has given breath his praises may be sung. That is the wish that finds voice in this petition. Is there anything that we can do toward bringing it to pass?

Most of the prayers that we offer we have something to do with answering. Can we help to answer this one? Assuredly we can, and it is one chief part of our duty as children of the Heavenly Father. The old catechism says that man's chief end is *to glorify God* and enjoy him forever. And there is much that we can do to show forth the honor of his name, and make his praise glorious.

1. We cause his name to be hallowed in the earth by telling the truth about him. When, by his indwelling in our own lives, we are enabled to think true and worthy thoughts about him, then we may tell these thoughts to others. The truth about him, when it is known, can only add to the lustre of his name. And one reason why many men do not hallow his name is simply that they do not understand his character. They have been told many things about him that are not true. If the things that they have been told *were* true, they could not glorify him in their thoughts, they could not even respect him.

Coming out of a place of worship some

time ago, I met a man in a very angry frame of mind. The preacher had been representing God as acting upon certain principles that are palpably unjust and wrong — as doing things that any civil magistrate would be execrated for doing. "If that is the kind of God that you people worship," said the angry hearer, "I wish to know nothing more about him." Of course I could do nothing else but tell him that the statements of the preacher, though made in good faith, were incorrect; that God was never known to act upon the principles imputed to him. But it was certainly a very unfortunate thing that this preacher, who was a good man, should have represented God to his hearers in a way that caused the moral sense of some of the most thoughtful of them to revolt. You are not hallowing the name of God when you make statements about him which give the impression that he is unjust or tyrannical or cruel. The truth about him will not make such an impression of his character upon any rational creature. Let us be careful, if we wish to promote the honor of his name, to say nothing about him that is not true.

2. We can cause his name to be hallowed, also, by showing men that we honor and love him. Good sentiments as well as bad sentiments are contagious. A sincere and honest reverence for God will communicate itself to other minds. If our neighbors see that we do hold his name and character in high regard, they will be inclined to feel that he is worthy of the honor we give him.

I saw once in Broadway, from a window where I sat (and the thing has been seen more than once), a cluster of men standing and looking at a certain quarter of the sky for an hour or two. What were they looking at? Nobody seemed to know exactly. The general impression was that they were trying to see one of the planets, Jupiter or Mars, which was bright enough to be visible by daylight. Who had gathered this group? Nobody. Two men had stopped on the sidewalk and had begun to look steadfastly into the sky. Presently some one joined them, and another and another, all looking in the same direction, some shading their eyes, some rolling their newspapers into telescopic tubes and peering through them. Not many questions would be asked by the members of such a group in New York; but somebody conjectured that it was a star that they were looking for, and said so, and that conjecture was passed from one to another, and served as the only organic idea that the assemblage possessed. The two men whose curiosity, whether real or feigned, was the origin of the collection soon passed on; nobody stayed long, but as one after another walked away with a puzzled or amused expression of countenance, their places would be filled by others who would be drawn into the little circle by the force of what the phrenologists would call imitativeness, — by the simple disposition to do things which we see other people doing. This was the only cause of this little shifting group of men and boys that kept its place for a good while in the busy street, into which some hundreds of men must have been drawn, and which caused thousands who did not pause to cast their eyes upward in the same direction.

Now, if this principle of human nature can produce such a striking result with so slight materials, it can surely be made to serve the higher interests of truth. If so many men can be made to look up into the sky so steadfastly when there is nothing to be seen, simply because they see others gazing that way, they who look up steadfastly into heaven and behold the glory of the Lord may be able to turn the eyes of others in the same direction. The unconscious influence of reverent hearts and praising lives will help to lift the thoughts of others to the same sublime realities.

3. Of praising lives, I said. For it is not chiefly by the reverent demeanor and the

devout speech of God's children that the glory of their father is promoted, but by the fidelity and nobility and beauty of their conduct. We who offer this prayer profess to be his children. "Our Father," we say. That is an acknowledgment of our relation to him, of our duty to him. If we proclaim that he is our Father, then those who do not acknowledge him will look to see what manner of spirit we are of. Children are expected to resemble their parents, in their characters as well as in their features. And if in our lives men see the purity and truth, the manliness and honor, the fidelity and charity that do belong to all who learn of him and abide in his fellowship and are transformed into his image, they cannot help honoring him in whom we live and move and have our being. "The Christian," Professor Christlieb says, "is the world's Bible." The Christian shows men in his own life the beauty and the loveliness of the divine nature. And we who pray that God's name may be hal lowed and held in reverence can answer our own prayer in no more effectual way than by keeping our lives so clean and bright that they may reflect his glory.

This first petition of the Lord's Prayer, without saying anything about it, deals a most effective blow at the central evil in human nature — our selfishness. Men are apt to be nearly as selfish in their religion, nearly as egoistic in their prayers, as in any other part of their lives. But this petition turns their thoughts wholly away from themselves. "Our Father who art in heaven," we say; and now that our thought is lifted up to the Infinite Giver what shall we ask for first? For the easing of our pains, the supply of our wants, the pardon of our sins, the saving of our souls, the welfare of our friends? No; these are things to ask for, but not first. "Hallowed be thy name!" Away from ourselves to God our thought is quickly turned. "Begin to pray," this petition says, "by ceasing to think of yourselves; by remembering that your small personality is not the centre round which this universe revolves. "Seek first the Kingdom of God and his righteousness," is the Master's great command, and here he frames it into the first petition of the prayer that is to be always on our lips.

After this manner therefore pray ye. Self must be the fulcrum on which your prayer will rest, but it is not the power that lifts you heavenward. It is by looking out, and not in, by looking up, and not down, that a man escapes from the bondage of sin into the liberty of the sons of God.

III.

THE ETERNAL KINGDOM.

Thy Kingdom come. — MATT. vi. 10.

WHAT is the Kingdom of God for whose coming we are taught to pray in this second petition of the Lord's Prayer? The phrase is used with a variety of meanings in the New Testament, sometimes in a narrow sense as signifying phases of individual experience, sometimes in a large sense as including all that the world has known or can know of the power and the love of God. We must suppose that the phrase is used here in its largest sense. It is not likely that in so brief a prayer as this any partial meaning would be given to the words employed.

The orthodox Jews had a very narrow idea of what the Kingdom of God was to be. They thought that it was simply a political machine to be set up at Jerusalem — a monarchy, with a King designated by divine power, under which the autonomy of the Jewish nation would be restored, the Romans banished from the Holy Land, and the territorial inheritance promised to Abraham occupied by his descendants. This was what they were looking for; this was the Messiah's Kingdom as they conceived and expected it. Certain Pharisees with this thought in their minds came to our Lord one day, and demanded of him when the Kingdom of God should come. He answered them and said, "The Kingdom of God cometh not with observation." "Comes not," as Robinson explains this phrase, "so that its progress may be watched with the eyes." "Neither shall they say 'Lo here! or, lo there!'" "None shall be able," says Alford, "to point here or there for a proof of its coming." It is not a matter of locality. Palestine is not the territory of its dominion; Jerusalem is not the seat of its power. "Behold the

Kingdom of God is within you!" "The Saviour," says Olshausen, "withdraws the Kingdom of God wholly from the local and phenomenal world and transfers it to the world of spirit."

This, then, is our Lord's answer to the Pharisees; and it may be instructive to many in this day whose faith clings to a material kingdom, who are waiting to hear some one say "Lo here! or, lo there!"

"The Kingdom of God," says Paul in his letter to the Romans, "is not meat and drink." No; and it is nothing that subsists on meat and drink. Flesh and blood do not inherit it, neither in this world nor in the world to come. The throne of its empire, the weapons of its warfare, are not carnal. What is it, then? "It is righteousness and peace and joy in the Holy Ghost." That is Paul's definition of the Kingdom of God. The Saviour tells us where it is. It is not in Jerusalem; it is not visible anywhere to mortal eyes; it is unseen and spiritual. It is within you.

Paul tells us what it is. It is not meat and drink, — it is not any material or earthly organization with a visible head; it is righteousness and peace and joy in the Holy Ghost.

The Kingdom of God is then in its essence a spiritual Kingdom; the seat of his dominion is in the thoughts and affections of men; the tokens of its sway are a deepening purity, and a growing love among the children of men. Of course it takes hold on things outward, also, and shapes them by its law, as we shall see by and by; it changes the manners and the fashions and the laws and the social relations of men; it is not in its essence meat and drink, but it rules the lives of men who are its loyal subjects whether they eat or drink or whatever they do. Still it affects the forms and fashions of life only as it transforms the thoughts and the desires of men; it works from within outward; its forces are all spiritual, though its manifestations are visible in all the realms of life. And it includes everything that is true, everything that is pure, everything that is lovely, everything that is honest and brave and sound and sweet in the universe. Whatsoever is good is of God, and is a sign of the rule of his Kingdom in the world. Whatever shows improvement — whether it is from good to better, or from worse to better — is a token of the progress of God's Kingdom in the world. Wherever morality and purity are gaining, wherever the vile are becoming less vile, and the cruel less cruel, and the covetous less covetous, there the Kingdom of God is advancing. "There is none good but one, that is God," said our Lord himself; and there is no good in any man, from the feeblest virtue in the worst man to the grandest integrity in the best man, — there is no good in any beneficent institution or in any kindly custom or in any refinement of social life, — that is not a divine inspiration; that is not the result of obedience to the divine law; that is not, therefore, a token of the presence and the prevalence in some degree of God's Kingdom.

When we intelligently offer this petition, then, we are asking for nothing less than this — that the light and love and power of God may increase and abound everywhere in the world.

I do not think we have the right to give the words any narrower meaning than this.

"God's Kingdom is here already, then," some one may say; "why should we be taught to pray for the coming of it? To say 'Thy Kingdom come' is to imply that it is not here."

To this question various answers are given. To one of the most common of these we have referred already. When we pray, "Thy Kingdom come," some say we are praying for the second coming of Christ. But they who thus distinguish between the Father and the Son must remember that this is a prayer which the Son bids us address to the Father. If there is any difference between the Father's Kingdom and the Son's Kingdom, it is the

Father's Kingdom and not the Son's whose coming we here supplicate. Besides, as it has been intimated, we can hardly suppose that this special sense would be given to a petition meant to be as comprehensive as this one. It is far more natural to give it a broader meaning.

Others say that this is a prayer for the organization of Christianity. The Kingdom here intended, says one learned commentator, is "the Messiah's Kingdom, which in organized form had not yet come, but was proclaimed by the Lord himself as at hand." But I do not think that our Lord ever cared so much for organization as to make the fashioning of a form of church government one of the main things to be prayed for in so short a prayer as this. No doubt organization is important; but it is altogether secondary, and secondary things are not provided for in this prayer. Besides, the church was organized in Jerusalem after the Pentecost, and it has always had an organization since. Whatever other defects may have been charged upon it, it has not often been deficient in organization since that day. It has generally had machinery enough, far too much. So that this petition must have been practically obsolete ever since the days when the first seven deacons were chosen. If, when we say "Thy Kingdom come," we mean only "Let thy church possess an organized form," we are praying an utterly superfluous prayer. For there are few of us who could honestly ask that the church have any more of organized form than it has to-day. One great trouble with it is, that it has so much more machinery than power.

To suppose, then, that the petition only asks for the return of Jesus Christ in a bodily form to earth, or for the organization of his church, is to give it a meaning altogether inadequate. It must have that larger and more spiritual meaning which we have already found in it.

"But why then," the questioner persists, "should we say 'Thy Kingdom come?'" If God's Kingdom is the sum of all beneficent forces, of all holy influences, of all truth and all love and all righteousness, why should we pray that it may come? It is here already. The world has never been wholly destitute of righteousness. God has never been without a witness on the earth. Purity, truth, and love have always had a place on this planet. If they belong to the foundations of God's Kingdom, then God's Kingdom has always been here since the morning-stars first sang together and all the sons of God shouted for joy. Why then do we pray "Thy Kingdom come?"

Why do we wish or ask in these days of March that summer may come? That would surely be a proper wish and might be a fitting prayer. Yet all the elements of the summer are here to-day. The earth, from whose fruitful breast the summer springs, lies waiting here; in her veins a myriad lives are throbbing; the mighty prince of light whose kiss is to waken all this life is shining down on us every day; air and light and moisture and warmth, all the forces that make the summer, are here; every day the sun is wheeling his chariot a little higher into the sky; every day the empire of the light enlarges, and the realm of night is narrowed; yet, though the elements and forces out of which the summer comes are here, we might wish to have them here in greater fullness and in greater power.

If we should make our illustration more specific it would not be any less pertinent. Take the sunlight itself, the great source of physical life upon this planet. It is here, it has been here, who knows how many ages? The tribes of earth have been rejoicing in its beauty and nourishing themselves upon its vital heat since the mists of the world's early morning first broke above its watery wastes; yet we do not cease to desire that the sunlight may continue to come. We have it, but we still have need of it; there will never be a season when we can dispense with its life-giving influence.

Now the analogy between these two relations — that of the kingdom of life on earth to the sun, and that of the Kingdom of righteousness on earth to God — is very close. And if it is lawful and rational to pray to the Father in heaven that he will continue to send his sun upon the evil and the good, then it is lawful and rational to pray " Thy Kingdom come! " If the first prayer does not necessarily deny that the kingdoms of life are already established on the earth, the other does not necessarily deny that the spiritual Kingdom of God is already established on the earth.

The petition asks, then, not that righteousness and peace and joy in the Holy Ghost may begin on the earth, for they begun to be long ago; but that they may continue, and that they may increase. Probably it is the increase of this Kingdom that is more specifically intended. It is a fuller, a broader, a more glorious manifestation of these great principles and forces. It is a prayer that the lives which are not now under their sway may be brought into subjection to them; that the institutions that now are ruled by selfishness and strife may be pervaded by them; that the homes in which vice and greed and worldliness now reign may be cleansed and hallowed by the spirit of purity and love; that the societies in which frivolity and vanity now rule may be ruled by soberness and modesty and quietness; that many lands which are now habitations of cruelty may hear and obey the gospel of good-will.

It is not a prayer that the leaven may be brought and placed in the measures of meal, but that its subtle, transforming influence may extend until it shall pervade the whole lump. It is not a prayer that the mustard seed may be planted, but that its growth may be hastened by the gentle dews of God's grace and the sunlight of his truth until it shall become a great tree whose branches shall be vocal with the songs of Paradise, and in whose shade all the weary of the world may rest.

This is, then, the most comprehensive petition of the Lord's prayer. Indeed it is the most comprehensive petition that it is possible for man to utter; there is hardly anything that we ask for that is not summed up in this prayer. It is a prayer that the whole world may grow better and brighter; that all the people in the world may grow gentler and stronger and truer and kinder and happier year by year. And it is a recognition of the fact that this can come to pass only as the world is filled with the knowledge of God and ruled by his law; only as the people in the world come to know him better and to obey him more perfectly.

It is a prayer that has been answered too, how many times, and how abundantly! People sometimes question whether prayer is ever answered; but here is a prayer that Christians have been offering now for eighteen hundred years, and if you want to know whether it has been answered read the whole of history since Christ ascended.

"Thy Kingdom come!" the disciples prayed; and presently a bloody persecution fell upon them in Jerusalem, and drove them forth from the Holy City and made them homeless wanderers. That was a strange way of answering the prayer. But "they that were scattered abroad went everywhere preaching the word." Up and down the rugged roads of Palestine they went proclaiming the glad tidings of great joy. It was not long before the messengers found their way over the heights of Mount Taurus, and here and there a centre of light was kindled in the dark provinces of Asia Minor; then the voice came to Paul summoning him to Macedonia, and Europe was invaded by the intrepid apostle, who planted the standard of the Gospel on the classic field of Philippi and on the heights of the Areopagus. From these small beginnings the leaven of Christianity has spread, until now nearly a third part of the human race acknowledge Jesus Christ as Lord.

This is simply putting into three sentences the story of the outward progress in the world of that specialized and organized manifestation of God's truth which we call the Christian religion. And while we freely admit that these peoples that are now called Christian are far from comprehending Christianity in its highest excellence and beauty, we may safely say that there is not one among them to which Christianity has not proved a blessing; not one whose darkness it has not enlightened, whose life it has not lifted up; not one in which there is not more of righteousness and peace and heavenly hope and joy than there would have been if the people had not heard of the coming of the Son of man.

But the progress of God's Kingdom in the world has not been confined to Chris tian lands, nor even to the Christian era. It is a prayer that devout men have always been offering and that God has always been answering. When Gautama Siddhartha, in the Indian city of Kapilavastu, four or five hundred years before the coming of our Lord, learned and taught the great renunciation, the Kingdom of God drew near to all those Eastern lands. For though the doctrines of Buddhism are but a partial revelation of God's truth and love, and though the rays of light that were mingled with its darkness have been greatly blurred by the perversions and corruptions of later days, yet there was truth in it, and the truth in it was God's truth; and there was love in it, and it was God's love shed abroad in the heart of Gautama; and it lifted millions of people up to a higher and purer life, and there was more of righteousness and more of peace and more of holy joy in their hearts and in their homes because of it and therefore we know that it was not wholly the kingdom of the evil one, but the Kingdom of God that Gautama Siddhartha, in some blind and imperfect way, was building. God had some better thing for us than he had for either Jews or Buddhists; but he had some good thing for them too; and the light that they saw, though it shone through many mists of superstition, was a beam from the Eternal Sun of righteousness. And so in other lands, Christian and Pagan, God has been preparing the ways by which his Kingdom may come into the world, by which it may enter and take possession of the lives of men and work from within outward in their languages and their laws and their arts and their social customs.

"Thy Kingdom come!" good Christians prayed. And he who hears the cry of his children came down to earth and stretched forth his hand to woman, so long the slave of man's power, and the drudge of his indolence, and the victim of his passions, and lifted her up, and clothed her motherhood with dignity, and her womanhood with di vinity, and gave us by her hand the blessing of home, the best of all earth's precious things.

"Thy Kingdom come!" the strong of faith were crying; and a Presence unseen by men stood among the prisoners in the dungeons that were festering dens of disease and vileness, and laid its gentle hand upon these hapless children of the evil, and lifted the weight of hate and scorn that made their lot so desperate, and sought to lead them forth to ways of purity.

"Thy Kingdom come!" God's children cried; and the victims of insanity saw a beam of hope through the mental darkness in which they were walking, and found themselves no longer chained and scourged like criminals, but gently led and kindly treated.

"Thy Kingdom come!" was the voice of millions who groaned in slavery, and of millions more who remembered their brethren in bonds as bound with them; and one by one the fetters have snapped asunder,—

the strong shackles of the Roman law, the wounding cords of feudal villenage, the degrading toils of British slavery, the prescriptive manacles of Russian serfdom, — until even in our own land, and in our own day, —

" Our eyes have seen the glory of the coming of the Lord,"

as he comes proclaiming liberty throughout the land to all the inhabitants thereof.

"Thy Kingdom come!" the children of the light were pleading; and the hierarchies that sought to confine the thought of men were baffled and paralyzed, and the Bible was unchained, and the ways that lead to the mercy-seat were opened to the feet of all penitent believers.

Thus it is by these mighty changes which have liberated and elevated and enlightened the children of men that God's Kingdom has been coming through all the ages, with increasing glory and enlarging power. Sometimes we hear the voice of his herald crying, "Who is this that cometh from

Edom, with dyed garments from Bozrah, glorious in his apparel, traveling in the greatness of his strength? He who hath trodden down the people in his wrath and trampled upon them in his fury." Sometimes the voice cries, "How beautiful upon the mountains are the feet of him that bringeth salvation, that publisheth peace!" But whether he come in his might with confused noise and garments rolled in blood, or whether he come in his gentleness, stealing in by all sweet influences to men's hearts, and kindling in them better wishes and kindlier feelings, — he is always coming; and the prayer that his children night and day are lifting to his throne is answered speedily, — yea with the light of every sunrising and the smile of every watching star.

And now, we come to ask whether there is anything we can do toward the answering of this prayer. Truly we can do much and in many ways. "Though the greatest,' says Mr. Ruskin, " it is that everlasting Kingdom which the poorest of us can advance. We cannot hasten Christ's coming. ' Of the day and the hour knoweth none.' But the Kingdom of God is as a grain of mustard seed; we can sow of it: it is as a foam-globe of leaven; we can mingle it: and its glory and its joy are that even the birds of the air can lodge in the branches of it."

Even the children can help to bring, in many places, this Kingdom of God for which they daily pray. I heard a mother telling the other day of her children who had quarreled sometimes, as many children do, I fear, but who had both been made so thoroughly sorry and ashamed on account of one of their quarrels that they were careful for many days after that not to say a bitter word, or to do a hateful deed. So peace came to that home through the prayer and the watching of these two Christian children ; and peace, you know, is one of the signs of the Kingdom of God in the world. And I hope that when the children offer this prayer they will remember that this is one of the ways in which it is answered, and in which they may help in answering it.

And wherever we help one another to the living of better lives, — to be more truthful or upright or honorable or kind, to be more faithful in our duties to God or to men, — there we are helping to answer our prayer, and to hasten the coming of God's Kingdom.

You offer this prayer sometimes, many of you, most of you, I trust. Do you always stop to think what it means? For it has a personal bearing. I have said that it is a very comprehensive petition, and so it is, but it has a very direct application to the life of every individual who utters it. It is like the " whosoever " of the Gospel; what makes it such a momentous word to me is the fact that it means *me*.

You pray that the Kingdom of God may come? Do you want it to come to Massachusetts? Do you desire that it should come to Springfield? Do you wish to have it come to your store, your office, your shop, your study, your table, your toilet, your closet, your heart?

How near to you do you desire that the Kingdom of God should come?

IV.

THE BLESSED WILL.

Thy will be done on earth as it is in heaven.
MATT. vi. 10.

THIS petition differs from the one which precedes it mainly in being more specific and personal. When we pray "Thy Kingdom come!" our thought goes more naturally to the whole grand result which God is working out in the world. We may and must think of the relation of this Kingdom to our own lives; but the primary suggestion is that of the universal prevalence of the Kingdom as an object of desire.

When we say "Thy will be done," the application to ourselves is more distinctly made. We think less of the whole than of the parts which compose it; yet we know that when the will of God shall be done by all that the Kingdom of God will have fully come.

This petition doubtless conveys to many of those who use it a lesson of simple submission. They suppose that it is the prayer of a passive rather than of an active faith. Mr. Ruskin says that many of the most earnest Christians always speak these words "as if their Father's will were always to kill their babies, or do something unpleasant to them."

Undoubtedly the prayer does include the thought of submission to the will of God. Sometimes the will of God conflicts with our plans, runs counter to our wishes, disturbs our repose, and then it is necessary that we should submit. In such times it is good for us to be able to say from the heart, "Thy will be done;" and therefore it is well for us to settle it in our thoughts beforehand that his will is a good will, and ought to be done; and that though for the present it may seem grievous, it is sure to bring forth the peaceable fruits of righteousness in all who trust Him, and wait upon his word.

There is a mistake just here, however, against which we must be watching. It is possible to be too submissive. Submissiveness may degenerate into supineness. We ought to be measurably sure that the ills that threaten us are coming upon us by the will of God before we submit to them.

A man is sitting upon a steep hill-side in the spring-time when he hears a noise, and, looking up, perceives a huge rock that has been loosened by the frost rolling down upon him. It is evident that the rock will pass directly over the place where he is sitting, and though there is time for him to escape he sits still, saying, "It seems to be the will of the Lord that I should perish here, and his will be done." But this is not the will of God in the truest sense of the word. The will of God is that the man shall escape; the noise that warns him is the call that summons him to escape; his sitting still is not trusting God, nor submitting to God, but tempting God most wickedly.

A man is suffering from dyspepsia, the result of his own imprudence in the use of food; or from nervous headache, the result of an intemperate indulgence in tobacco; and though he does not mend his habits, we hear him talk in the midst of his sufferings about being submissive to the trial God has put upon him. All suffering, he says, comes from the hand of God; it is his will that I should suffer; his will be done. But it is not God's will that this man should suffer; this is not the portion that God has chosen for him; it is the portion that he has chosen for himself. He is altogether too submissive.

The income of a family is cut off and they are left in distress. They make some efforts to find employment and livelihood, but they do not readily obtain what they seek, and presently they settle down into what seems to them a pious resignation to the decrees of Providence, but what their neighbors think is utter shiftlessness. I have known a number of families that were quite too submissive to what they called the will of the Lord. More grit and less resignation would have kept them in better circumstances.

It is only in a secondary sense that suffering can ever be said to be the will of God. His will is expressed in his laws; obedience to his laws brings health and happiness and peace; disobedience brings suffering. His will is that men should obey his laws; but that if they do not obey they shall suffer. The suffering is a warning against disobedience, and a dissuasive from it.

It is true that men are so linked together by ties of hereditary and of social organization that suffering may come upon me as a result of the disobedience of my ancestors or of my neighbors. Sometimes by diligence and patience I can reach the causes of this suffering and remove them; when I can that is my duty; when I cannot, then right reason and filial trust call on me to submit.

Suppose I come into the world with a hereditary tendency to consumption or paralysis, the result of the disobedience of some of my ancestors to the laws of health. Now it may be possible for me, by prudence and temperance, to counterwork these tendencies and to preserve and confirm my health. There are remedial and restorative forces in my physical system that may repair the damages that have been entailed upon me, if these damages are not too serious. It is my business to give these remedial forces a chance to do their proper work. They are the highest and most perfect expression in my nature of the will of God; and it is this part of the will of God that I must be most careful to have done.

But it is possible that the injuries which I have inherited are so serious that the natural remedial forces will not repair them, no matter how great care I may exercise; when this is so I must submit. Shall I say that the suffering which I endure as the consequence of these inherited injuries, by which my days are burdened and my life is shortened, comes upon me by the will of God? Yes; there is no other way of explaining it. It is in the nature of things that disobedience should bring suffering not only to him who disobeys, but often to his children and his children's children for many generations; and the nature of things, as Mr. Joseph Cook says, is "the total outcome of God's free choice." The universe is so made that sin not only inflicts but entails suffering; and God made the universe. The suffering that is inherited is not, however, penalty; it is no sign that God is displeased with me; it may be a means of grace to me, if I will rightly use it. And this is where the duty of submission comes in: the patient endurance of ills that cannot be mended is a part of the divine discipline in which we must all be exercised. There are plenty of pains and infirmities and troubles that we are not to blame for, and that we cannot help; we may not always understand the reasons of them; but we do know that the God under whose wise laws they are visited upon us is infinite Love, and that in some way, if we rightly use them, they will work together for good to us; and therefore, in the midst of such suffering, we are ready to say to him, " Thy will be done."

There is room, then, in the Christian experience for submission, and reason enough why we should often put this passive sense into this petition. But I am afraid that we often provoke our Heavenly Father by substituting submission for obedience; by lying still and piously taking the consequences of disobedience, instead of rising up and obeying; by *enduring* his will in the shape of penalty, instead of studying and doing his will, as it is made known to us in the laws of the universe, and thus avoiding the penalty.

A city is suffering from some epidemic; one family after another is invaded by the destroyer, and the mourners go about the streets. In the midst of the sorrow, many devout expressions of submission to the will of God are heard. But this scourge is not, I say, in the deepest and truest sense of the word, the will of God. His will is that people shall find out and obey the laws of health; they suffer in this way, only because they fail to do his will. The epidemic is not his first choice for this people, but his second choice; it is not the result of an arbitrary decree; it is conditional upon their disobedience; the epidemic results from causes for which men are responsible, and which men are bound to find and remove. And over every such suffering community, where the black shadow of the pestilence darkens the homes of the people, and the faces of men are pale with fear, the infinite Compassion is brooding, and the infinite Patience is crying, "I have no pleasure in the death of him that dieth, ... wherefore turn yourselves, and live ye!"

They who do the will of the Lord, then, please him far more than they who *suffer* his will; and the principal meaning of this petition is that God will help us in *doing* his will, rather than that he will give us patience in enduring the sufferings that result from disobedience. That qualifying clause of the petition to which we have not yet referred makes this very plain. "Thy will be done *on earth as it is in heaven.*" But it is not by endurance and submission that the will of God is done in heaven. It is not in sorrow and bereavement that the angels and the just men made perfect sit down in the mansions above, saying, "Thy will, O God, be done!" In heaven God's will is not enforced as penalty upon his children; there is no need of that; it is *done* by his children. And it is not done by them as a servant does his master's will, but in a free, hearty, loving, intelligent, obedience. The voice of him who said " Lo I come; in the volume of the book it is written of me, I delight to do thy will, O my God: yea thy law is within my heart," is the voice of all that glorified company. This is the very definition of heaven. Heaven is that place where all the creatures of God know and do his will; therefore there is and can be for them no sorrow, no pain, no death. Being conformed to his will they are made partakers of his nature, and thus enter into peace and blessedness and everlasting life.

Now, we are taught to pray, "Thy will be done as in heaven, so in earth,"— as by angels and the glorified, so by mortals. This means not endurance, but intelligent and joyful obedience.

I am sure, my brethren, that we have not given sufficient emphasis in our religious life to this meaning of the petition. Our religion has been occupied far more in seeking to save us from the consequences of disobedience, than in seeking to understand and obey the will of God. Doubtless we have all disobeyed God's will, and are not only suffering the present consequences of disobedience, but are also exposed to other and more serious consequences in the future: doubtless it is necessary for us to study how we may escape from these; but after all it is no more important that we should be delivered from the penalties of past disobedience than that we should study to be obedient in the present. A child who was always trying to evade punishment for past offenses, or beseeching you to forgive them, and who yet kept right on recklessly disregarding your commands, would seem to you neither filial nor dutiful. Penitence and reconciliation on account of past misdeeds are well, as far as they go, but they must not take the place of present obedience.

Let us try to remember, then, that our religion ought to show us not only how we may be forgiven for not having done God's will in the past, but how we may do it in the time to come. Let us remember that God is better pleased with us when we are doing his will than when we are suffering the consequences of disobedience, or when we are suing to be forgiven.

To do God's will we must know what it is. How shall we find it out?

The first and most obvious answer to this question is that his will has been revealed, and that we find it in his Word. And if we remember that the Bible is the history of the moral progress of the Jewish nation out of barbarism into civilization under the Divine guidance, and that many of the commands given were accommodated to the low moral condition of the people, and contain, therefore, an imperfect morality; if we remember that it is in the teachings of Christ, who fulfilled the law in righteousness, that the perfect revelation of the will of God is to be found, then that answer may stand. The Bible does make known to us the will of God, only let us be sure that we know how and where to look for it. Some of the commands of the Bible are local and temporary; even some of the principles incorporated into the ancient legislation are obsolete. They belonged to the scaffolding with which God was building his temple and not to the temple itself. But there are also many commands of the Bible that are of universal obligation. The words of Christ, as I have said, are the perfect utterance of God's will. And those holy men who were taught by Christ himself, and who were inspired of God to teach and preach his Gospel, have given us in their Epistles, and especially in the last chapters of them, in which they teach of practical religion, a clear expression of God's will, In the thirteenth chapter of First Corinthians, for example, you will find a revelation of God's will as distinct and perfect as it is possible to put into language. The same thing is true of the twelfth chapter of the Epistle to the Romans, and the third chapter of the Epistle to the Colossians, and the sixth chapter of the Epistle to the Galatians, and the whole of the Epistle of James, and many such passages. I am not saying that the whole Bible is not profitable for doctrine, for reproof, and for instruction in righteousness; I am only pointing out those portions of it in which that part of the will of God which we ought to do is most clearly set forth.

Our Lord himself has condensed the whole of God's law into two short commandments: —

"Thou shalt love the Lord thy God with all thy heart, and with all thy soul, and with all thy mind," and, —

"Thou shalt love thy neighbor as thyself."

He who perfectly obeys these two commands perfectly does God's will.

So then we find in this Holy Book such a declaration to us of the will of God as may serve to guide our feet into the ways of obedience. If we study the Word with a prayerful and teachable mind, we shall know more of his will than we shall ever find time and strength to do.

"But is there not danger that men will misunderstand these teachings of the Bible?" some one asks. "May they not often interpret these words to mean what they do not mean? Is it not true that different persons and different sects give to these words various and even contradictory meanings?" Yes; to a certain extent that is true. Still I do not think there has been so much dispute concerning the *will* of God, as revealed in the Scripture, as concerning the *methods* of God's working. It is the philosophy of religion, or the forms of religion, that men quarrel about more than the principles and rules of conduct. It is not concerning what God requires *of them* that they disagree, so much as it is concerning what his thoughts and counsels and purposes are for the whole universe. And the fact is that if these wrangling sectaries would make it their main business for a little while just to find out that part of the will of the Lord which they can surely know and which they ought to be doing, — and then would do it, — all the disputing and quarreling would speedily come to an end.

It is not, then, so difficult as some may think to find to find out, by reading the

Word of God, what God's will is. No one will go far astray who applies his own common sense to the task of finding in the words of Christ and of his apostles what the Lord would have him to do. But he may have a better guide than his own common sense. It is not necessary that he should lean wholly to his own understanding. That may mislead him. He may have the enlightenment of the Holy Ghost as he studies the Holy Word. A sanctified common sense is a safer interpreter of the Word of God than learning and genius unsanctified.

Following this guide, therefore, we may find in the Bible a bright revelation of the will of God. And if, in all our study of the Bible, we sought this mainly — to find things to do — to get hints as to the kind of work God has for us, in the cleansing of our lives, and in the serving of him and of our neighbors in the world; if we went to it as to an order-book in which we expected to find some definite direction for the doing of God's will to-day, — I am sure that our study of the Bible would do us much more good than it now does. We are too apt to read the Bible and study the Bible as a mere perfunctory service. It is a thing to be gone through with, there is so much Bible reading or Bible study to be done; it is a duty, and when it is done it is done, like any other duty. Or else we fall into the habit of thinking that there is a certain charm about it; that the study of the Bible in some mysterious way has a kind of alterative effect upon the character; so that to spend a certain time every week reading it will prove to be a means of grace. If we could get rid of all such formal and superstitious notions, and just remember that our main business with the Bible is to find out from it what God wants us to do, the book would speedily come to have new meaning and value.

I do not think that I have exaggerated the importance of the Bible as a chart for the guidance of men in doing God's will.

Mr. Matthew Arnold is not much of a believer, but he says that conduct is three fourths of life, and that the Bible, far above all other books, is the book of conduct. We shall be safe, I am sure, in adopting his maxim, so that while we pray "Thy will be done," we may search the Scriptures to find each day how to help in answering our prayer—what part of God's will we ought each day to be doing.

But while the principles on which we ought to act are clearly set down in the teachings of Christ and his apostles, and while many applications of these principles are suggested also in the Word of God, our study of nature and of providence ought to throw much light upon the ways in which these principles are to be worked out. For God's will is revealed not only in the Bible, but also in nature and in providence. We learn the will of God as we learn the will of a man, not only by attending to what he has said, but by observing what he is doing. His works quite as distinctly as his words indicate his will.

So when I pluck in the meadow a violet or a crow-foot bloom, and look it in the face and see how deftly its petals are carved and how daintily they are painted, then I learn a little of what God's will is. Such a thing of beauty as this is an expression of his thought and of his love. He no more wills that I should be holy than that this flower should be beautiful. And although the flowers are not all perfect; although in an unkindly environment some of them have been maimed and scarred; yet of this we are always sure, that the flower which is most beautiful comes nearest to being the flower that God meant to make and did make in the beginning.

So when we see a human being of good stature and fair proportions, with a clear eye and a ruddy skin, and the wholesome beauty that springs from perfect health, we are able to say with equal assurance that God's will is revealed in the body which that soul inhabits, however poorly it may be done by the inhabitant. And though there are many decrepit and diseased bodies in which human beings make their homes, yet we are sure that those bodies which are soundest and most symmetrical and most beautiful are the nearest like what God means all the bodies of men to be.

In like manner when we meet with a human life that is upright and modest and pure and beneficent, based on firm principles of justice and honor, working quietly but energetically for the building up of righteousness, — we know that God's will is revealed in such a life as this more perfectly than any words can tell it, more clearly than any flower can show it, more fully than the shapeliest form and the comeliest face can reveal it.

And when we go into a home in which love is the law, in which each member of the household seeks to live worthily, and in which all conspire together to seek one another's welfare and happiness, so that the law of the home seems to be, Each for all and all for each, — then we are sure that God's will is made known to us in the life of this household; that something like this is what he would have every home to be.

And if we should find ourselves in a community where peace and order and temperance and thrift and industry and contentment abounded; where there was no squalid poverty, and no filth-breeding pestilence, and no enormous fortunes, and no profligate expenditures of wealth, and no extortionate capitalists who kept themselves wholly aloof from the work-people by whose labor they were enriched, and cared not, so long as their dividends were undiminished, how fast the laborers were pauperized and brutalized, where there were no eye-servants, that worked only when they were watched, and no discontented and surly and suspicious employees; where the law of good-will had prevailed over the law of supply and demand, making peace where once was strife, and spreading plenty where once was poverty, — if we ever should find such a community as that we should know of a surety that God's will had found expression in its corporate life; we should say with confidence that every community on earth would be like this community when his will should be done on earth as it is done in heaven.

In short, my friends, we know that God wills that beauty and health and symmetry and vigor and virtue and courage and charity and fidelity and tenderness and love and joy and peace and good-will shall increase and abound everywhere on the earth; and that whenever we plant a seed in the secret place that will bring forth such fruit as this, or whenever we say a word or do a deed that will lead to such result as this, we are helping to answer this prayer. Answered it will be in God's own time, in God's own way. His will shall be done everywhere upon the earth as it is done in heaven. He never taught his children to offer a prayer that he did not mean to answer. It only remains for us to put ourselves in line with the divine purposes, remembering that this prayer is not the voice of supineness and quietism, but that the words are fit to hold all the energies of our greatest hopes and our strongest volitions. Let us learn here on earth, not only to *endure* God's will, when it thwarts our plans and takes away our pleasures, but to *do* his will with swift and glad obedience, as it is done by strong angels and happy saints in heaven.

V.

THE CONVENIENT FOOD.

Give us this day our daily bread. — MATT. vi. 11.

WE come now to the first petition of the Lord's Prayer that expresses a personal want of the petitioner. By all that has gone before this we have been taken out of and away from ourselves; we have lifted up to God the voice of reverent and filial love, acknowledging him as our Father; we have prayed that his *Name* may be honored and sanctified in the thoughts of men; that his *Kingdom* of righteousness and peace and joy in the Holy Ghost may be established and promoted; and that his *Holy Will* may be done in earth by men as it is done by saints and angels in heaven. We have not thought as yet of our own necessities. If we have wants we have not considered them, and half of the prayer is said already

Our minds have been led away over the universe of God; we have been made to take in the great purposes of the divine love, and the great attributes of the divine character; and now with this preparation we come to think of our own personal needs. Plainly, we shall not be quite so selfish, quite so insistent, quite so querulous in our petitioning as we should have been if we had not been lifted up and led forth along these higher paths.

"Give us this day our daily bread." Shall we use these words literally, or shall we give them a spiritual signification? Is it food for our bodies or for our souls, or both, that we ask for in these words? I incline to the opinion held by the majority of expositors that the petition is to be taken in the plainest sense; that it asks for a supply of food for our bodies. This is indeed one of the primary necessities. Light and air God gives us freely; after these indispensables food comes next in order of importance; and this is not, ordinarily, made ready to our hand in nature. Some labor is necessary to procure it, some care to husband it; it becomes an object of thought and desire as light and air do not; and therefore it is something to be prayed for. Our Lord teaches us to pray for it; and in this petition we have a clear warrant for praying for temporal mercies. Surely if it is lawful to pray for a thing as common as daily bread, it is lawful to pray for anything we need. We may not see how God can give us these gifts we ask for without working a miracle, but that is no reason why we should refuse to ask for them; he is able to do for us exceeding abundantly above all that we ever ask or think.

1. The first thought suggested, then, is that of our dependence on him to whom we pray. Every good and perfect gift is from him — this one, surely, not less than the rest. For health to earn our daily bread, for wisdom to keep it and use it, we de-

pend upon his goodness. The habit of connecting our commonest gifts with the great Giver is a habit that we may well cultivate. It is thus that life is sanctified and ennobled. "Take away this divine symbolism from our material existence," says James Martineau, "and let it stand only for what it can make good on its own account, and what is there to redeem it from selfishness and insignificance? The home sinks into a house, the meal into a mess, the grave into a pit." Our daily bread is not a thing too little for God to give, nor too vulgar for him to bless; and when with reverent faith it is thus received as a gift from him, the breaking of it is a sacrament, and the real presence of the infinite love is in the heart of the man who partakes of it with thanksgiving.

2. For daily *bread*, we are bidden to ask. The word is specific, not generic. It signifies, primarily, *bread*. There is another word which means food in general.

The use of this word in this place seems to hint that it is only for plain and simple food that we ought to make our requests unto God. It is not, Give us this day our bill of fare, — our daily three courses; it is, Give us this day our daily bread. It is a prayer that the epicure would hardly think of offering. And while we need not adopt any ascetic theories about meat or drink, we may surely attend to the suggestion conveyed in this petition of a simple and wholesome diet, and may endeavor to make our practices tally with our prayers

3. Give us this day our *daily* bread. The word here rendered daily has been the subject of much curious discussion, and with good reason; for it is not found anywhere else except in the Lord's Prayer. It does not occur in any other place in the New Testament, and it is not used by any other Greek writer. The meaning of it can only be inferred from the etymology, and the interpretation which seems to me most sat-

isfactory makes it equivalent to sufficient or necessary. This meaning does not alter the force of the petition as we always understood it. To say "Give us this day sufficient bread" is precisely the same as to say "Give us this day our daily bread." The prayer is to be offered every day, and it asks only for that which will suffice for the day. The lesson that is thus conveyed is one of moderation in our wants. We are not to ask for abundance or superfluity, we are to ask only for what we need. We are not to pray for banks- or bins- or barns- or cellars-full, but only for our daily bread.

You will notice that this is the only petition in the Lord's Prayer in which temporalities are mentioned, and our normal desire concerning them, which is put into words by our Lord, hath this extent, no more. Just imagine the average American trying to put his wishes for worldly good into these simple words! The things that he craves, that he is striving after, that in his inmost soul he is praying for, — how vast and multiform are they when measured by this humble petition! What he would say if he spoke his mind in his prayers would be: "Give me this day my daily ten per cent.!" or "Give me this day a booming trade!" or "Give me this day a chance to make a thousand dollars!" With his mind full of these vast schemes, of these eager ambitions, imagine him kneeling in his closet in the morning and taking upon his lips this prayer: "Give us this day —— our daily bread!" What a little thing that is to ask for, compared with the things that he wants and is working for! To what a small scale this prayer is drawn! How can he bring his inflated speculations, his racing ambitions, within the compass of this simple prayer?

It will be hard for him to do it, no doubt; yet it will be well for him to try. To remind himself thus, every day, of the plan of life that God has for him — of the moderate and frugal temper in which God means that he shall abide — will be instructive and may be salutary. If he thinks what this petition means when he utters it, he will not be in quite so much haste to get rich when he rises from his knees; he will come a little nearer to understanding that a man's life consisteth not in the abundance of the things which he possesseth.

"But are we to take these words in strict literalness?" some one asks. "Does this petition forbid forethought and thrift? Must we desire nothing beyond the supply of the actual wants of the present day? Is it wrong for us to lay by us in store something against the time of need?"

No; I do not think we can put quite so much meaning as this into these words. I do not suppose that our Lord meant to contradict the counsel of the wise man, who bids the sluggard learn of the ant a lesson of providence. The virtue of thrift is in many ways directly and indirectly enjoined and commended in the Scriptures.

But the fact is that this prayer is very short, and it is meant to express only the primary wants of men. There are other things of value, but their value is secondary. Sufficient food to sustain life is a primary want; that is indispensable; some store in the cellar or bank, something laid by against a rainy day, — that is well; we may wish and work for that, and pray for it too, I think; but it is of secondary importance. It is not to be named among the indispensable things. We will take it, if it comes, and be thankful for it; and pray for wisdom to use it worthily; if it does not come, we can be content without it.

The petition, then, calls only for that which is absolutely necessary, and teaches us to school our cravings for material good into soberness and moderation.

4. "Give us this day *our* daily bread." It is *given* to us, and yet it is ours. We receive it from the great Giver as a benefaction, yet we have a certain sort of proprietorship in it. How does it become ours? What is it that gives us the right to speak

of it as if it were a possession? Is it ours only when we appropriate it? Is it ours as the children's bread is theirs — provided for us, and set before us, and only ours when we partake of it? No; I think there is a deeper meaning than this. God does not, as a matter of fact, give us food in this absolute way; and I do not believe that he wishes us to ask him to provide it for us in this way. Our daily bread is to be ours, we are to make it ours, in quite another sense than that in which the infant makes the food that is fed to him his own. *Our* daily bread — the daily bread of all who are able-bodied adult persons — is ours when we have earned it; when by our own labor we have provided it for ourselves. If we are children, too young to work, or if by reason of sickness or age we are unable to work, then we may thankfully take the food that the love of others provides for us. But it is well even for the children to remember that they can do something toward helping to earn their daily food; that the little tasks and errands of the household which they are competent to do take just so much of burden from the shoulders of the father and mother by whose labor they live; and that they cannot very consistently offer this prayer unless they show themselves ready and willing at all times to do these little services that are within their powers. Their daily food will be somewhat sweeter to them, I am sure, if they have the consciousness that it is not wholly won for them by the toil of their parents, but that they have helped a little in earning it. It is not good for children to feel that they are *wholly* dependent; the sentiment of honorable self-support ought to be bred in them from their earliest days. As they are constantly sharers in the good that is gathered for the household, so they ought to be sharers, in some wise measure, in the labor and care by which it is provided.

"Give us to-day *our* daily bread," means then, and can only mean, when it is spoken by healthy men and women, — "Give us a chance to earn our daily bread by some kind of honest work." We wish to eat *our own* bread, not some one else's. Bread that we beg is not ours; bread that we take as lazy pensioners on some one else's bounty is not ours; bread that we steal is not ours; bread that we get from other people by fraud and extortion and over-reaching is not ours; only the bread that we have earned by honest work and fair traffic is ours. "Give us this day *our* daily bread."

Now just think what a revolution would be wrought in our social and industrial and commercial life, if everybody devoutly offered that prayer and lived up to it every day! How many idle hands for which Satan is all the while finding mischief would be set to work. How much of greed and fraud and craft and cruelty would at once come to an end!

Certain it is that there are large classes in our civilized society who do not intend to eat their own bread and who do intend to eat every day bread that belongs to somebody else — bread that they have either begged or stolen, or procured by fraud or extortion.

There is first a considerable number of grown-up boys and girls in our well-to-do families who are out of school, who are in absolute idleness, and who have made no strenuous effort to find anything to do. They do not wish to earn their daily bread. They greatly prefer to subsist on that which their parents have earned and saved for them.

There is also another class of paupers, a little lower down, who are not ashamed to beg, and who mean to subsist upon the gifts of the town almoner, or upon the benefactions of the charitable This class has been growing very fast of late in all our larger towns and cities.

There is another class of people who pretend to work, but who mean to do just as little as they can; who never intend to give a fair day's work for a fair day's wages if they can help it; who will shirk and slight and botch everything they do, caring only to draw their pay when pay-day comes, caring nothing at all for the interest of those who employ them. Those who employ labor have a sorry sense, sometimes, of the prevalence of this spirit among those who work for hire. Such people cannot honestly ask the Lord to give them their daily bread; it is not theirs that they are trying to get, but their employers'.

All those people who get their living by ministering to the vices of their fellow-men belong in this category. The money that is paid for vice is money that ought to be paid for daily bread, for things useful and necessary. Somebody needs it; somebody suffers without it; and he who takes it and gives in exchange for it the means of vicious indulgence is taking somebody else's daily bread, and giving nothing for it so good as a stone, — nothing better than a scorpion. If he lives by such traffic as this he never eats his own bread. Think of a man who keeps a tippling shop praying every morning, "Give us this day *our* daily bread." It is not *his* daily bread that he means to eat; it is the bread that belongs to the haggard wife and the pale-faced children of the man to whom he sells the daily or the hourly dram.

All those persons who get their living by gambling, whether it be in gold or stocks, or wheat or corn, must be ranked in the same class. Gambling is not a productive occupation. It adds nothing whatever to the world's wealth; it does nothing whatsoever to facilitate exchanges; its whole effect is to unsettle values and keep business feverish and dangerous. The men who follow this nefarious avocation render the community no service at all; the world is not enriched materially or mentally or morally by anything they do; by no stretch of charity can they be said to *earn* anything. Yet there is an army of them, and they get daily bread — many of them a **good** deal more than that. It is not theirs in any honest sense of the word; it belongs rightfully to somebody else; every dollar that they gain makes somebody a dollar poorer and nobody richer in anything under the heaven. I should not wish, then, to hear any man who gambles in securities or in bread-stuffs saying "Give us this day our daily bread," for I should know that he did not mean what he said; that he meant to eat mine, or some other man's, and not his own.

Then there is a class of greedy capitalists, proprietors of great companies, managers and stockholders of large corporations, employers of labor, to whom this prayer would be little better than blasphemy. Understand, that I am not speaking of *all* capitalists or organizers of labor, but *only* of those who prove by their deeds that they have no compassion on the poor; that they mean to make their eight or ten per cent. even though to do it they are obliged to cut the workman's wages down to a point at which it is hard for him to get the daily bread for his children. I know that some companies and some employers are quick to share with their laborers their increasing profits, and slow to reduce wages even when profits turn to losses; but there are others, I am sorry to say, who even in times of prosperity crowd labor down to the starvation point, heaping up their profits by the impoverishment of the people who do their work. And if I should hear such a man saying this prayer I should want to answer him: "My dear brother, do you not know that God knows that you are not speaking truth when you speak these words? Do you not know that you are *not* content with *your* daily bread, with what you have fairly gained, but that you mean to rob these poor people who work for you of a part of *their* daily bread? Of course you will not do it by meeting the man in a dark lane, as he is returning from his labors, and knocking him down and taking his loaf out of his basket and running away with it; you will do it in strict accordance with the laws of the state and the law of supply and demand; you will simply take advantage of the crowded labor market, and drive a sharp bargain with workmen who are nigh to perishing."

It is not, then, for any of those who prey upon their fellow-men — whether they do it by the law or in defiance of the law — to offer this petition. He who sincerely prays that God would give him a chance to earn his daily bread by honest labor prays at the same time that other men may have an equal chance. "Give *us* this day *our* daily bread," the prayer is: not "Give *me* this day *my* daily bread." And the spirit of the petition not only rouses me to work for my own livelihood; it also forbids me in any way to hinder or prevent my neighbors from gaining their livelihood; it forbids me to eat my bread in idleness, in the sweat of other men's faces, or by the debauching of their lives.

5. There are some among us who may

seem to be absolved by their circumstances from the duty of offering this prayer. Here is a man whose larders are full, whose cellars are crowded, whose barns are bursting with gathered grain, whose bank account shows a daily balance of many thousands, — is it not a little superfluous for him to say this prayer? Can he ask without stammering that the Lord will give him this day his daily bread when he knows that he has enough in his possession not only for this day but for many days to come? Should not those whose provisions are so ample, whose accumulations are so vast, skip this petition when they offer the Lord's Prayer? Is it not something like mockery for them to take these words upon their lips?

No; I do not think so. Notice again that it is not "Give *me my* daily bread," nor is it "Give me and my household our daily bread," it is "Give *us* this day *our* daily bread." Who are included in these plural pronouns? How many are there of

" us "? Just as many as are included in the first word of the prayer. That "our," we said, takes in all mankind. So do the pronouns of this petition. You cannot give them any narrower meaning. This prayer throughout, in every one of its phrases, identifies you with all humanity. The man who wishes to pray only for himself and his immediate family and friends must make his own prayer; the Lord's Prayer will not serve his purpose. You cannot intelligently use it and keep your thought fixed upon your own individual necessities, or on the needs of your own household. He who thoughtfully takes these words upon his lips takes at the same time all human wants by sympathy upon his own soul, and craves the outpouring of the infinite bounty upon every needy human brother.

Kneel, then, O you who have much goods laid up for many years, kneel in your closets and around your family altars and lift up to the heavenly Father this prayer.

Think! when you utter it, not only of those who surround your table, — think of your neighbors too. Some of them are toiling hard for small wages, and find it not always easy to keep the wolf from the door; some of them, though willing to work, stand idle in the market-place because no man has hired them; some of them are sick and helpless and those who lean on them are destitute; take them all into your thought, fold the arms of human brotherhood round them all, and then say, "Give *us* this day *our* daily bread." Your neighbors — they do not all live in the wards of your city; who are your neighbors? Every human being is your neighbor. From other lands beyond the sea sad tales of famine come to your ears; hunger and cold are blanching the faces of little children; while you bow before the throne of the All-bountiful these swarms of starving wretches will come into your thought. Let them come in! Make room in your hearts for all of them, and then say again, speaking for them more than for yourself, "Give *us* this day *our* daily bread."

I care not how vast your possessions, how abundant your stores, this prayer is for you. Humbly, thankfully, heartily utter it, and then say each one to himself, "Is there nothing that I can do to help in answering this prayer? Cannot I be God's almoner to one or two of these needy and famishing thousands? Cannot *I* give *this* day in Christ's name daily bread to some who are perishing without it, or, better still, can I not help some of them to find a way of earning it for themselves?"

I do not think, my friends, that I have strained one word of this petition beyond its natural and obvious sense in my interpretation, and surely we have found a great deal in it, far more than I ever thought was in it before I began to study it. No one can intelligently offer this petition without learning from it, whenever he utters it, a lesson of humble dependence on

God for daily mercies, — a lesson of frugality, a lesson of self-support, a lesson of equity, a lesson of charity. All that is in it and comes naturally out of it so soon as we begin to think of what the words mean. It is a prayer for rich men quite as much as for poor men ; but it is a prayer that no man can utter, without deceit and mockery, who does not mean to do justly and to love mercy, — that ought to blister the lips of any man whose deeds show that he is willing to live by begging or shirking or cheating or stealing, or by preying on the vices or the necessities of his fellow-men.

God help us all to live so that it shall not be mockery to say, every day, —

"GIVE US THIS DAY OUR DAILY BREAD!"

VI.

THE FORGIVING GRACE.

And forgive us our debts as we forgive our debtors.
MATT. vi. 12.

"THERE is one very simple lesson," says Mr. Ruskin in his comment on this petition, "needed especially by people in circumstances of happy life, which I have never heard fully enforced from the pulpit, and which is usually the more lost sight of because the fine and inaccurate word 'trespasses' is so often used instead of the simple and accurate one 'debts.' Among people well-educated and happily circumstanced it may easily chance that long periods of their lives pass without any such conscious sin as could, on any discovery or memory of it, make them cry out in truth and in pain, 'I have sinned against the Lord.' But scarcely an hour of their happy days can pass without leaving, were their hearts open, some evidence written there that they have 'left undone the things that they ought to have done,' and giving them bitterer and heavier cause to cry, and cry again, forever, in the pure words of the Master's prayer, ' Forgive us our debts.' "

The word trespasses is used by the Master himself a little later in this discourse, in explaining this petition: " For if ye forgive men their trespasses, your heavenly Father will also forgive you. But if ye forgive not men their trespasses, neither will your Father forgive your trespasses." Yet, as Mr. Ruskin says, the word debts is more exact and more comprehensive than the word trespasses. It includes both kinds of faults, — the things done and the things left undone. The contrast is not quite so strong between the two Greek words for which these words stand; but the English trespass, on account of its use as a legal term, conveys to most minds the notion of an encroachment upon other people's rights and one who asks to have his trespasses forgiven may think when he prays only of such overt and injurious deeds as these. But debts are duties owed to God and man, owed and not paid, — and those who live the most quiet and inoffensive lives must find, if they stop to think about it, such liabilities as these weighing heavily upon their consciences.

It is also well to recall a truth that ought to be familiar, — that in Christ's own representation of the judgment to come it is these duties left undone, rather than any crimes done, that furnish the ground of condemnation: "I was hungry, and ye gave me no meat . . . . Inasmuch as ye did it not."

It is our neglect, then, as well as our transgression, our idleness as well as our violence, our indifference as well as our extortion, our apathy as well as our excess, our coolness as well as our hate and scorn, for which we here pray to be forgiven.

The key word of this petition is the little word *as*. "Forgive us our debts *as* we forgive our debtors." We ask not simply to have our offenses and deficiencies forgiven; we ask to have them forgiven in a certain way, according to a certain rule or standard. In Luke's version of the prayer the phraseology is different, but the meaning is the same: "Forgive us our sins, *for* we also forgive every one that is indebted to us." The forgiveness that we ask for is compared with and conditioned on the forgiveness that we grant. We forgive those who have wronged us, *therefore* forgive us. *As* we forgive those who have wronged us, *so* forgive us."

That may seem a hard and impracticable rule, but that is the rule. Whenever you offer the Lord's prayer you ask that the *kind* of forgiveness you mete to others shall be measured to you by the Father of mercies.

Let us see how this rule will work in a number of such cases as are occurring every day.

"That man has wronged me," says one, "and I never can forgive him. I have no purposes of revenge; I will let him alone if he will keep out of my way; but the wrong that he has done me is irreparable, and it is useless to ask me to overlook it or make light of it. I will not forgive him."

Well, my friend, that makes it a pretty serious thing for you to say the Lord's Prayer. "Forgive us our debts," you say, "as we forgive our debtors." Forgive me the wrong I have done, just as I forgive the wrong this enemy of mine has done to me; which is, being interpreted by your unrelenting grudge, "Forgive me not at all; forgive me never." That is a fearful prayer to offer; but it is exactly what the Lord's Prayer means in the mouth of every man whose heart holds an implacable resentment.

"I can forgive my enemy," says another, "I will always treat him well; but I never can forget the injury he has done me. The recollection of that wrong rankles in my breast, and I could not forget it if I should try."

This, then, is the spirit in which you expect your heavenly Father to deal with you. You wish him simply to let you off, to quash the indictment against you and set you free; but you expect him to keep always in mind the wrongs that you have done, and never to think of you without thinking of them. The sort of forgiveness which is expressed by the common saying, "I can forgive, but I cannot forget," is not a very liberal sort; bitterness and wrath are mixed with it; do you want wrath and bitterness mingled with God's forgiveness of you? That is what you ask for when, with this spirit in your heart, you take this prayer upon your lips.

"I am ready to forgive him," says another, "when he is ready to be forgiven. It will be soon enough for me to grant him pardon when he asks for it."

But suppose that your heavenly Father had followed this rule in his treatment of you, and of all mankind. Suppose that he, upon his throne of holiness and justice, had said: "It will be time enough for me to be reconciled to these sinful and thankless children of mine when they seek to be reconciled. When they repent of their transgression and ingratitude and return to me with contrite hearts, I will show my grace to them and not before." If that had been the divine purpose from the beginning, where now would the race of men have been, and what would have been the outlook for you and me? It was not the grace that waits for contrition and confession, but the grace that goes before them and prepares the way for them, that saved sinners. It was when we were enemies that we were reconciled to God by the death of his Son. The largest and best part of God's forgiveness is that which precedes man's repentance. Do we mean to say to him, in our prayers, that this antecedent and unsolicited grace of his, which overcomes our enmity and wins our confidence, is superfluous and nugatory? Is this what our petition means, "Give us always the mercy that we ask for and no more." We are sinning every day, and it is the goodness of God that leads us to repentance. Do we wish, in our prayers, to announce to God that we will have none of this goodness? That is precisely what our prayers mean when we say that we will grant our pardon only to those who sue for it, and then pray, "Forgive us our debts *as* we forgive our debtors."

It is plain that this announcement of a common measure between the human and the divine forgiveness, this declaration that men can only ask for the kind of pardon that they are ready to grant, is, in itself, a rather startling word from God to men.

"The mercy I to others show,
That mercy show to me,"

is the substance of this petition; and none but a good man can offer it without calling down wrath upon his own head. I fear that there are not many of us who would not be filled with fear, if we thought that we were really going to be forgiven by our heavenly Father *in just the same way* that we have been in the habit of forgiving those who have injured us. And if the forgiveness that we supplicate from him must be the same as that which we extend to others, it is high time that we began to ask ourselves what kind of forgiveness it is that we are wont to extend to others. We shall discover, no doubt, that it is often a surly and stingy sort of forgiveness; and we shall see that our method needs to be reformed altogether. By what standard shall we reform it? I know no better standard than that which is exhibited in the gracious dealings of God with his children.

For although, as I have said, we have no right *to ask* God for a quality of mercy that we are not ready to grant to others, yet God, of his infinite grace, shows us mercy far more full and free than we have a right to ask for; far more full and free than that which we show to others; if he did not it would go hard with us. Even with those of us who are full of spites and grudges he is patient and long-suffering; it is his abounding love that wins us out of our enmities. We can learn, then, what must be our temper, when we pray to be forgiven, only by studying the acts and attributes of him by whom we hope to be forgiven. When we see how God forgives we shall not only know how we ought to forgive others, but also in what mind we must be when we ask for his forgiveness.

This is no strange thing. We always learn what to ask for in our prayers by seeking to know what God has made ready for us. *That* is always the very thing we need.

If I could only succeed now in erasing from your minds all the analogies and figures that are borrowed from human governments to illustrate the divine government, the task of making plain the truth respecting the divine forgiveness would be greatly simplified. The governmental terms which are used in the Bible — sparingly there, however — have been laid hold of by theologians, and made to serve not only as the form of all sound doctrine, but even as the substance thereof. Everything that God does is brought under some kind of governmental act or operation; the rules of political expediency are supposed to explain all his dealings with the children of men. The maxims on which a human magistrate acts are assumed to be the maxims on which God acts; what a human magistrate can wisely do, God can do; what a human magistrate cannot wisely do, God cannot do. It would be difficult to invent any sort of contrivance that would more effectually befog the whole subject. For the fact is that the analogies of human government are utterly inadequate to explain God's dealings with men. The political rules on which the wisest and best human magistrate must act are wholly unlike those on which God acts;

the canons of expediency that he must observe do not limit infinite wisdom and infinite power and infinite love. That a Being who is both omniscient and omnipotent is shut up to the methods of human magistrates is altogether improbable. Our governor could not pardon every criminal in our prisons who professed to be penitent, simply because our governor cannot tell who is penitent and who is not; every man of them would profess at once to be deeply contrite and radically reformed, and the great majority of them would return, on being set free, to their old ways. But if our governor could know absolutely (as he never can) that a certain man in our jail was thoroughly reformed in heart and life, and that, if he were released, he would always be a useful, upright, honorable citizen, then it would be the duty of our governor to pardon that man and set him at liberty. The law would not be honored by keeping any such man in custody a single day, no matter what his past life had been. The law is intended to secure righteousness, nothing else; it ought to be a minister of wrath only to them that work unrighteousness; it should not, and if it is a perfect law it cannot, keep any man in condemnation who is now heartily, and who will henceforth be loyally, on the side of righteousness.

The most important limitations of pardon in the case of the human magistrate are, therefore, those which arise out of his ignorance. He cannot pardon the truly penitent, not because to do so would be any detriment to the state or any dishonor to the law, but simply because he does not know and cannot know who is truly penitent. Our human administration of law is at best but a clumsy and imperfect operation; and to argue from the methods to which it must in its feebleness resort to the methods of divine government is the depth of absurdity.

Suppose now you let go a little while of these governmental analogies and take hold of the thought which this prayer enforces, that God is our Father. Is it true that a father cannot, without endangering the welfare of the household, forgive an erring child whom he has good reason to believe to be truly penitent? Suppose one of my children transgresses one of my commands. I am in entire ignorance of the fact, and there is no prospect of its being discovered, but the conscience of the transgressor begins to work; he is sorry for his offense and ashamed of it; and by and by he comes to me and tells me all about it and asks me to forgive him. I have the very best reasons for believing that he is sincere in this, and that he will continue to be dutiful and obedient in time to come. Do you say that if I forgive this child without punishing him I shall undermine the family government? I say that I could in no other way so weaken the family government as by refusing to forgive him. I say that I could no more deny one of mine who came to me in this way than I could deny him food if he needed it. What sort of family govern ment would that be which would be undermined by the free forgiveness of a child who showed that he was not merely afraid of punishment, but heartily sorry for the wrong that he had done, and honestly determined to make all the amends for it in his power?

If, then, we simply forbear to force all our thoughts about God's dealings with us into the forms of human jurisprudence, and remember that the central and crowning truth of our relation to him is that he is our heavenly Father, we shall not feel that we are obliged in our theories to limit his power to forgive sinners who are truly contrite and obedient. There never was a moment since the worlds were made when God could not pardon any sinner who was heartily sorry for his sin, and desirous of walking in the ways of righteousness. To refuse pardon to such an one would be to doom him to continue in alienation from God. By such a refusal God would become the upholder and maintainer of sin. That he can never be.

I have been speaking, thus far, of only one phase of the great fact of the divine forgiveness, the lesser and lower part of it. What I have been speaking of is simply the release of the sinner from penalty — what is technically called pardon or remission of punishment. I have shown that God is willing and able to pardon any sinner who is truly penitent. And this, I suppose, is about all that is commonly meant by the divine forgiveness. But the divine forgiveness means a great deal more than this. For, as we have seen already, the forgiving love of God begins its work upon the sinner while he is yet an enemy, long before he is ready to ask for pardon. When he has come to this, that he is willing to ask for pardon, that work is well-nigh done. It is in the love of God, the free, unsolicited, prevenient grace of God that compasses him round and makes plain to him the peril of his evil ways, and sounds in his ears the offers of the divine compassion, and gently constrains him to repent and return to obedience and trust, — it is in this that we see what the divine forgiveness is. There is one New Testament word, translated forgive, that means all this. It does not signify simply to discharge an offender, to release from a penalty; it means to show grace unto, to deal grace upon, another. It suggests all that patient, loving work of kindness and self-sacrifice, by which the one who has been wronged seeks to gain the love of the one who has wronged him, and to reclaim him from his sins. The meaning which we must put into the word forgive when it represents this word is infinitely larger than that which belongs to it when it represents the other word, which only signifies to remit a penalty. Here is one of the texts in which we find the larger word: "Be ye kind to one another, tenderhearted, forgiving one another, even as God in Christ hath forgiven you."

Here then is the field in which the divine forgiveness begins its blessed work for men. Far back of man's contrition this grace is manifested. Man is not forgiven because he repents; he repents because he is forgiven. It is the goodness of God that leads him to repentance. What kind of goodness? God's providential favors merely? No; but the suffering and reconciling love of God in Christ.

"For we ourselves also," says the great apostle, "were sometimes foolish, disobedient, deceived, serving divers lusts and pleasures, living in malice and envy, hateful and hating one another. But after that the kindness and love of God our Saviour appeared, not by works of righteousness which we have done, but according to his mercy he saved us, by the washing of regeneration and renewing of the Holy Ghost which he shed on us abundantly through Jesus Christ our Saviour."

"And you," he says in another place, "that were sometime alienated and enemies in your mind by wicked works, yet now hath he reconciled in the body of his flesh through death, to present you holy and un blamable and unreprovable in his sight."

Such, then, is God's method of forgiveness. To those who are alienated from him and enemies *in their minds*, to those who are hateful and suspicious and scornful, he draws near, and, without forcing his love upon them, he lays loving siege to them, and by all the gentle ministries of his spirit, and all the marvelous tokens of his dying love in Jesus Christ our Lord, seeks to subdue their enmity and to reconcile them unto himself. He not only has a pardon waiting for every sinner who will accept it, but he is doing continually all that he can do, without breaking down the man's freedom, to change his stubborn mind and his rebellious heart, and make him willing to ask for the pardon that is waiting for him. This is God's way of forgiving.

And this, my friends, is the way that we want him to forgive us. We do not deserve all this love but we need it, and we cannot do without it. If it were not for this infinite compassion, this abounding grace, there would be small hope for us.

If God were only compassionate and kind to us when we were obedient and dutiful to him it would go hard with us. The only foundation of our hope is in the fact that he remembers us even when we forget him; that he is faithful to us when we are unfaithful to him; that he is patient with us when we sorely provoke him; that he follows after us when we go astray from him. This is the only grace that is sufficient for us; and surely it is nothing less than this abounding grace that we ask for when we pray to him.

Well, then, if we ask for it, we must be ready to extend it to others.

God's forgiveness includes self-sacrificing love, a giving of himself for sinners. If we are to be the children of our Father in heaven, if we are worthily to offer this prayer which Christ has taught us, we must be ready to give ourselves for those who have injured us.

Is this a hard saying? No harder than any other requirement of the perfect law of ove. It is the steady and uniform teaching of the New Testament. No doctrine ever fell from the lips of Christ or his apostles that conflicted with this prayer. It is, indeed, one of the rudiments of Christian morality. Alas, that there are so many Christians who have not begun to learn it! Yet I think we are getting on a little in our understanding of this virtue. Lord Herbert of Cherbury, a brother of the poet George Herbert, and an English nobleman of the seventeenth century, has a passage in his autobiography bearing upon this matter. "I am confident," he says, "that in the forgiveness of injuries no man of my time hath exceeded me; for though whensoever my honor hath been engaged no man hath been more forward to hazard his life, yet when with my honor I could forgive, I never used revenge, as leaving it always to God, who, the less I punish mine enemies, will inflict so much the more punishment on them." That is surely not a very Christian reason for forgiving one's foes. Other rea sons that he gives are also curious: "When a man wants and comes short of an entire and accomplished virtue, our defects may be supplied this way, since the forgiving of evil deeds in others amounteth to virtue in us; that therefore it may not unaptly be called the paying our debts with another man's money." The notion seems to be that forgiveness is a work of supererogation, and that it helps to balance the account of our sins. He comes a little nearer to a just view when he says, "That he that cannot forgive others breaks the bridge over which he must pass himself; for every man has need to be forgiven." We will trust that Lord Herbert's frank judgment that no man of his time had exceeded him in forgiveness was somewhat too favorable to himself; certainly we will hope that a good many in our time have somewhat clearer notions about it.

Yet I am afraid that there are few in these days, even of those who have long been members of the Church of Christ, to whom Christ's clear command, "Love your enemies; do good to them that hate you and pray for them that despitefully use you and persecute you," does not seem rather a visionary and doubtful maxim. But there is no commandment of his that is more nearly universal in its obligation, none that is to be more literally and exactly obeyed, none that reaches more directly the foundations of Christian character, none that is more evidently intended for every-day use. It is not only the few Christians of exceptional piety who are to love their enemies; it is one of the very first things expected of every disciple of Jesus Christ.

That word of Christ's about "gaining" a brother who has trespassed against you is a luminous word. That is the very thing to do. If his spirit is bad, if he is full of envy and malice, if the wrong that he has done you was cruel and unprovoked, these are the very reasons why you should conquer his hate by your kindness, thus losing a foe and gaining a brother. And a brother is worth gaining. Of all the gains we make none are so precious as those of friendship. To have secured one more wise and loyal friend is to have greatly enlarged your revenues. And a friend won in this way, one who has surrendered an unreasoning enmity to your victorious love, can hardly fail to be a friend forever.

Have you never gained with such weapons such a victory as this? Is there not one among your friends who was once your foe? And did you not find in the self-denials by which you gained him an exceeding great reward?

Some of you think that this is an enterprise that requires for the prosecution of it more grace than you possess. Do not think so poorly of yourself. Surely, if you have ever begun to learn of Jesus Christ, you can feel something of the strength of the motives that urge us to this service.

You find it hard to enter upon such patient and self-denying efforts to win the love of your enemies. You do not wish them any harm, you say; if you ever had purposes of revenge you have long ago dismissed these from your thought; you will even treat them courteously when you meet them; but to love them, to undertake in any way to show affection for them and to seek to change their enmity to love, — this you are not able to do. But consider, my friends. You say you do not wish these enemies of yours any harm; can you not go a little farther than that? Can you not truly say that you would shield them, if it were in your power, from any harm that threatened them? That man who has wronged you, — if you saw his house on fire, and knew that he was asleep within, would you not run and rouse him? You know that you would. You are not so base that you could stand by and see one who had injured you suffering and not interpose to save him if you had the power. You would despise yourself if you should permit even your just resentment against wrong to make you inhuman.

Now if you would take pains, and expose yourself to danger and loss, in order to save your enemy from death or physical damage (and any of you would do that, I am sure), why should you not be equally quick to save him from moral injury? Is not the evil that kills the soul worse than the evil that kills the body? Are not the wounds that a man suffers in his immortal part more grievous and fatal than those which he suffers in his mortal part? and if so, why should you not be at least as prompt to shield him from one as from the other? You own that it would be inhuman to let your enemy be roasted alive in a burning building if you had the power to rescue him; is it not equally inhuman to permit his better nature to be consumed in the tormenting flame of a rancorous and reasonless malignity, when you have the power to rescue him from that?

For you must not forget that this enemy of yours is hurting himself, sorely, bitterly, whensoever he does you wrong. He hurts you, it may be; but the harm he does himself is ten times greater than the harm he does you. When he tells a lie about you, the lie may injure your reputation somewhat; but how much more deadly is the injury that it inflicts on the soul of the man who tells it! He smites you in the face, wantonly and without provocation; but how much worse is the wound that the reaction of that rage inflicts upon his character! He must either hate and despise himself whenever he thinks of it, or else, nursing his blind passion, he must be preparing himself for darker moods and deadlier deeds.

Now, think of the harm that these enemies of yours are suffering as well as of the harm that they are doing. Can you not, as one who loves his kind, who is not pleased to see any human being hurt or maimed in any part of his life, — can you not at least pity these enemies of yours, feel for them a pity which has in it no mixture of contempt, but is a real and sincere compassion?

Are you so utterly egoistic in your emotions that your whole thought is fixed upon the injury that *you* have suffered in your dealings with them, so that you have no regrets left for them though they are suffering so much greater injury? No; I will not think so badly as that of any of you. If you have never found in your heart any compassion for your foes, it has simply been because you have never reflected upon the real state of the case; because you have never taken pains to put yourselves in their places and to realize to yourselves the terrible loss and detriment that they must be enduring. I know that when you think of it you cannot help being sorry for them, and that you will be glad to do what you can to save them from the destruction they are bringing upon themselves.

You will need, though, when you set forth on this enterprise, to be very prudent. If any man ought be wise as a serpent and harmless as a dove, it is the man who undertakes to gain his adversary. The more unjust and unreasonable he has been in his treatment of you, the harder it will be to win him. "We hate those whom we have injured," the Latin proverb says. The worse your enemy has wronged you, then, the worse he will hate you. He cannot help being angry with himself on account of the injustice he has done you, and this anger he will vent upon you also. There is nothing so illogical as ugliness. It is such a man as this, perhaps, that you have to win out of his enmities. It will not be an easy task. No officious peacemaking will do. If you should send him word, or tell him, that you had forgiven him and were going to do him all the good in your power, you would only make him all the angrier. Perhaps it will only be by stealth that you can serve him at first. You will need about as much ingenuity and tact and patience as would be required in taming a wild-horse or in tunneling a mountain. But, my friend, you can do it. By prayer and perseverance, by the aid of the wisdom that is given without upbraiding to every one that wants it, and the love that is shed abroad in the heart through Jesus Christ our Lord, you can conquer this hate, and make your enemy your friend. Did any better fight than this ever summon you to a worthier victory?

But perhaps you say to yourself: "The case is not, after all, so clear as the preacher is making it. I cannot conceal from myself the fact that this enemy of mine has grievously wronged me. This wrong has awakened in my heart a feeling of resentment. It is not altogether a selfish feeling. The indignation that stirs in me is, at least in part, a righteous indignation. I think that I do well to be angry when such wrongs are done, no matter who may suffer them."

Well, my friend, I allow that there is some force in what you say. I do not assert that these resentments of yours are altogether sinful. I believe that they are natural — would be natural to an unfallen and perfect human nature. But, after all, I do not think that these indignations ought to rule our conduct. They may speak, they will speak, but there is another voice that ought to be more commanding, and that is the voice of love. There is the man; he has been your enemy, but he is your brother. He has injured you, but he has injured himself more. If, in striking you a blow that did you no permanent injury, he had fallen and crippled himself for life, you would be magnanimous enough, I am sure, not only to keep no grudge against him but to seek to show him kindness. The case that he is in is no better than that. You may feel resentment toward him, but your feeling of pity, your desire to do him good, will be a stronger feeling. It is not by resentments that the man is to be won to better ways; wrath and indignation never changed any man's heart; it is kindness alone that will win him, and this is the work that God has given you to do. Every such unreasoning enmity displayed against you by any human being is a call to self-denying work in behalf of him who cherishes it. If you have any such adversary, you need not go about asking the Lord to show you some Christian work to do. There it is!

It is quite possible, however, that these natural resentments of yours, of which we have been speaking, will need a little chastening. Perhaps they will be so stern and loud that you can hardly take upon yourself any loving labor in behalf of your enemy. If so, it may become necessary for you to discipline them by some real self-denial. The opportunity may come to you of making a costly sacrifice for the man who has wronged you. Do not miss that opportunity. Not only may you thus subdue his enmity, you will quench your own hot indignations. You cannot keep on hating anybody for whom you have voluntarily endured hardships and made sacrifices. And it is not at all probable that he will keep on hating you. By giving yourself for him you will gain your brother; and in so doing you will not only execute your own purpose of forgiveness, you will also bring him into the better mind in which he can receive forgiveness.

And this takes us back to the central thought of the petition we are studying, that it is only when we are in this state of mind towards those who have wronged us that we can offer this prayer. We want from God a full and free forgiveness, that has mingled with it no grudges and no coolnesses; a forgiveness that blots out our transgressions, that takes away all our iniquity, and receives us graciously and loves us freely; and that mercy which we want from him we must be ready to show to others. We stultify ourselves by asking our heavenly Father to extend to us a measure of forgiveness that we are not willing to extend to our brother. Such a prayer is mockery, and we know that it is when we offer it.

What is more, we cannot receive the fullness of the divine forgiveness until we are ready ourselves freely to forgive — even to give ourselves for — those who have wronged us. The trouble is not with the phraseology of the prayer, but with the facts of the case.

You say that the desert is a desert because no rain falls upon it; but that is only half the truth. No rain falls upon it because it is a desert. The heated air rushing up from its arid surfaces disperses the vapors that would descend in rain. Some moisture there must be on the earth, else there cannot be rain from heaven. So in your heart this forgiving disposition must be, else you cannot rejoice in the fullness of God's forgiving grace. The pardon may wait in the sky above you, but it cannot descend to you until that mind is in you which was also in Christ Jesus.

In more than one impressive lesson Christ

enforced this truth upon his disciples. The parable of the unmerciful servant is one of these; and you do not forget that other word of his in the Sermon on the Mount: "If thou bring thy gift to the altar, and there rememberest that thy brother hath aught against thee, leave there thy gift before the altar; first be reconciled to thy brother, and then come and offer thy gift." The fact that all acceptable prayer must proceed from a forgiving spirit, that no man can be reconciled to God who will not be reconciled to his brother, is constantly and strongly asserted.

You have seen more than once clear illustrations of this truth in the lives of disciples. You have seen enmities and jealousies and grudges growing up between neighbors and brethren in the church; and in every such case you have noticed that the spiritual life of these quarreling Christians grew feeble and fruitless; that there was no fervor in their prayers, no joy in their praises, no sign of heavenly influence in all their holy convocations. And then you have seen a better mind take possession of them; mutual confessions and reconciliations followed; those who had been long estranged came together and forgave each other, and renewed the old bonds of charity and brotherhood. And then, how quickly, to the assemblies so long frigid and forlorn, the warmth of holy love and the consciousness of the divine presence returned; how the pulse of the church was quickened, and the new life from above issued in abundant fruits! Every great religious awakening is preceded by such works of reconciliation; and no wise servant of Christ expects any real spiritual growth or progress among those who are divided by petty feuds and contentions. It is not till we are ready to forgive that we find any profit in our prayers.

It is pleasant to testify that there are no unseemly and scandalous strifes among those to whom these words are spoken. Yet there are few of us, I fear, who cannot think of individuals with whom we have had some little dispute or disagreement, toward whom we are cherishing a feeling of dislike if not of enmity. And it may be that in the hearts of some of us there are bitter and angry feelings toward those who have wronged us, or with whom we have been at variance. Is it not a good time now to resolve that by the grace of God we will conquer these resentments, and compose these difficulties, be they small or great; that we will not harbor in our hearts an unkind feeling toward any man; and that we will not give over till we have won the love of those who most bitterly hate us? There is no comfort in these grudges; they mar all our pleasures and spoil all our peace. There is no good in hating or in being hated. It is no credit to any man to hang on to his resentments. Some people fear that they will demean themselves by showing a forgiving spirit, but it is a gaunt and ill-favored sort of dignity that lives on piques. You would better let it starve to death. There is no manlier endeavor, no enterprise more chivalric, than the conquering of a foe by loving him out of his enmity.

It is only thus that you can be the children of your Father in heaven, who maketh his sun to rise on the evil and on the good, and who sendeth his rain on the just and on the unjust. And it is only when this mind is in you that you can bow before his throne and say, —

"FORGIVE US OUR DEBTS AS WE FORGIVE OUR DEBTORS."

VII.

THE GREAT SALVATION.

And lead us not into temptation, but deliver us from evil.
MATT. vi. 13.

"SUPERFLUOUS and absurd!" cries the critic. "Why should I make any such request as this? You tell me that God is the infinite Goodness. Surely I cannot believe in any God to whom righteousness in his creatures as well as in himself is not the supreme concern. Now I am bidden to beseech this Being of infinite holiness not to lead me into temptation, not to place me in circumstances where my virtue will be seduced and overcome. It is impossible that he should do anything of the kind. What says the apostle: 'God cannot be tempted of evil, neither tempteth he any man.' If he does not tempt us himself, is it likely that he will lead us into places where evil spirits of men or angels will tempt us? It is absurd to suppose that he will, and it seems like insulting his goodness to ask him not to do it."

This objection seems rational, and if the word temptation in the text always meant what the objector supposes it to mean, it would be much more difficult to answer. But the word in this place has quite another meaning. The verb from which it is derived signifies to test, as well as to tempt. It sometimes signifies to assail one's virtue by deceit and seduction, with the intent and purpose of overcoming it; it sometimes signifies to prove one's knowledge by examination, or to test one's character by wholesome discipline, with a benevolent rather than a malign purpose.

Let me give you some instances in which the word is used in this latter sense. When Jesus saw the five thousand men gathered about him on the further shore of the sea of Galilee, he said unto Philip: "Whence shall we buy bread that these may eat

And this he said to *prove* him, for he himself knew what he would do." The word "prove" in this place is the word often rendered "tempt." "Examine yourselves," says the apostle, "whether ye be in the faith." The word "examine" in this text is the very same word. "I know thy works," says the Lord to the church at Ephesus, "and thy labor and thy patience, and how thou canst not bear them which are evil, and hast *tried* them which say they are apostles and are not, and hast found them liars." The word tried, in this text, is the same word.

This, indeed, is the primary meaning of the word. It signifies to try, to put to the test. And you may put a thing or a person to the test for a good purpose or a bad purpose; to put a character to the test for the purpose of subverting it is what we ordinarily mean by temptation; to put a character to the test for the purpose of bringing out its latent powers, and confirming its virtue, is a method to which

God does, no doubt, in his wisdom, sometimes resort.

It is true that the same experience may be to one an improving test and to another a hurtful temptation. From the same ordeal one man will come forth invigorated and elevated in purpose and thought, another debauched and demoralized. The result of this trial depends on the man's own moral fibre. And I suppose that God never by his providence leads any man into the presence of a trial which the man is not strong enough to resist, or which he does not give the man strength to resist. "God is faithful, who will not suffer you to be tempted above that you are able; but will with the temptation also make a way to escape, that ye may be able to bear it."

Any trial, then, may be a temptation to one whose moral nature is sickly and whose will is weak. Every pain may be a temptation to one of small courage and fretful temper, — a temptation to murmur and repine. Every small loss, every slight disap pointment, every little discomfort, may be a temptation to the peevish spirit and the feeble will, — a temptation to surliness and gloom. Relatively to such natures as these half of the inevitable events of life are temptations; yet most of us would be slow to pronounce every change in the weather and every mischance of daily life a temptation. Some measure of hardship we expect to encounter in this world, and in cheerfully bearing it or wisely ignoring it we obtain a needful discipline. That God does place us in the midst of such trials as these and keep us among them we know very well; it never occurs to us to accuse him of tempting us by this measure of exposure. And those to whom the inevitable and ordinary trials of life, the little pains and grievances and slights and losses, are temptations, can never offer this prayer, "Lead us not into temptation," without meaning by it, "Take us out of this world straightway; take us immediately to heaven!" For existence in this world is not, and will not be in our generation, exempt from such trials as these. They are the constant accompaniment of life. They are inseparable from our environment. They furnish every human being who is not a moral imbecile with opportunities of improvement rather than occasions of sin. And when we remember that God's grace is vouchsafed to all who will receive it, to enable them to profit by these providential trials, we shall surely feel that it is a gross use of language to speak of them as temptations, and that the human being to whom they are temptations is a faithless and pusillanimous creature. To ask God to lead us away from everything that tries our patience, that tests our endurance, that disciplines our faith and courage, is simply to ask him to relieve us of the burden of existence. We do not pray for this. What then do we mean when we pray "Lead us not into trial?"

We mean, to begin with, that while the ordinary providential discipline through which we are passing is welcomed by us as a means under God's hand of growth in virtue, yet that there are sore trials that we shrink from enduring, and into which we beseech our heavenly Father that he will not conduct us. We mean by it just what Paul meant, when from suffering that came to him in God's providence he besought the Lord thrice that he might be relieved, and heard for answer, " My grace is sufficient for thee; for my strength is made perfect in weakness." The suffering was wisely ordered, no doubt; and yet I suppose that Paul did well to pray to be delivered from it. Suffering is not a good in itself; it may sometimes be a means of good, but in itself it is an evil. Every perfect human being naturally wishes to be delivered from suffering. He will patiently endure it if he must, if there are ends of character to be gained by enduring it, but it is natural and right to shrink from it. Those who crave it as a good in itself, who come to feel that suffering is meritorious and praiseworthy, have imbibed a morbid and heathenish notion, as unlike the Christian idea as any notion can well be.

They who pray "Lead us not into trial" are offering the very same prayer that our Lord himself offered in Gethsemane: "If it be possible let this cup pass from me; nevertheless, not as I will but as thou wilt." It was the natural human shrinking from extreme suffering that found utterance in this petition. There was no halting of the will before this ordeal; the "nevertheless" modifies the natural desire, and brings it into subjection to the judgment and the will. Once before, standing in the very shadow of the cross, our Lord lifted up the same cry, "Now is my soul troubled and what shall I say? Father, save me from this hour. But for this cause came I unto this hour! Father, glorify thy name."

With these words of Christ in our memory, those of us who believe in him will have no difficulty in believing that it is not wrong for the holiest and most devoted man to pray to be delivered from severe trials. Trials there are that tax the endurance and the courage of the strongest hearts; it is not only no sin, it is but imitation of the example of Christ Jesus our Lord, to pray to be shielded from them. Only we must always say what he said, "Nevertheless, not my will, but thine be done." "Father, glorify thy name!"

There are feeble and faithless spirits, as we have seen, to whom the smallest troubles are temptations; to almost any of us a *great* trial might be a temptation. Upon the bravest of us a blow might fall that would blot the brightness from our sky and banish the gladness from our homes,— a trouble so sore that we should be tempted to doubt and complain, and rebel against God. To every finite spirit there is a breaking strain. And it is right for us to pray that God will mercifully save us from these extremities of trial.

Do you point me back to what I said a little while ago, — that we know beforehand that God will not lead us into any straits from which he will not graciously help us out? True; and that is precisely what this prayer asserts, as I understand it. The second phrase, of which we have not yet spoken, must always be connected with the first. Lead us not into trial, *but* deliver us from evil. Is not that an exact parallel of our Lord's own prayer already quoted: "If it be possible let this cup pass from me; nevertheless, not my will but thine be done!" Lead us not into trial; but, if trial must come, keep us from falling into doubt and sin. Let not our trials prove temptations, but with the trials give the grace to bear them, so that they shall be ministers of good to us, and not of evil.

In this view of the petition, then, it is a simple, natural expression of desire that the Lord would mercifully lead us not into, but away from, the furnace of affliction in which souls are sometimes tried; and a devout recognition of the fact that if, in his wisdom, such suffering must come to us, it is in his grace alone that we can trust to keep us from the evils of doubt and despair and rebellion against God.

But the meaning of the petition must be somewhat extended. Doubtless it includes not only the endurance of suffering, but also the resistance of moral evil; and it asks not only that the Lord will spare us great trials, but that he will also shield us from the assaults of evil wills.

Much of our environment is not of God's devising. Bad characters, bad associations, bad influences, fill many of the paths that open before our feet. Indeed, it is impossible wholly to avoid the evil. The child that is most carefully watched, the youth whose ways are most circumspect, the man who keeps his soul most diligently, comes into frequent contact with sin; and the truth which this prayer recognizes is that this contact with the evil is not to be sought, but shunned. It recognizes the fact that every man has his weaknesses and limitations, and that it is safer for him to be surrounded with good influences than with evil influences; that character grows better in a congenial than in an uncongenial atmosphere. We must encounter evil; our daily duty will bring us often face to face with it; but some paths are safer than others, some associations are less hostile to virtue than others; and the prayer is that God will lead us into those paths where the danger is least; that, so far as it is consistent with duty, his kind providence will keep us out of associations where our virtue will be assailed. To ask God that he will not lead us into such exposures is not to imply that he is likely to do this and must be besought not to do it; it means, simply, lead us out of and away from temptation. The petition contains something like what the logicians call a negative pregnant, in which the negation of one thing implies the affirmation of the opposite.

The petition implies that God will lead us if we ask his guidance.

It also implies that if we will follow him he will lead us into safe places and away from the snares that are set for our feet.

It expresses our desire to be kept, so far as we may be without neglecting duty, from exposure to the allurements of vice and sin; to be surrounded with virtuous rather than with vicious influences.

It confesses our faith that God will so keep us if we put our trust in him.

The true Christian purpose and practice is suggested by this prayer, and it is a golden mean that lies between two extremes.

The one extreme is that of the religious recluse, who, because of his fear that his life may be tainted by the sins of the world, withdraws himself wholly or mainly from intercourse with his fellows. If he does not retire into a monastery he turns his home into a cloister, shuns society, and wraps his robes closely about him when he walks the crowded streets. We know that this is not the Christian way of living, because it is not the way that Christ himself lived, and his last prayer for his disciples was, "I pray not that thou shouldst take them out of the world, but that thou shouldst keep them from the evil." What he desired for them was, not that they should be shut out from all association with their fellows, but that they should be kept from being harmed in their characters by such associations.

The method of his kingdom is personal contact and influence. It is by the friendly association of the good with the evil, by the communication of truth and love from the good to the evil, that the evil are to be saved, and the world redeemed. The leaven in the lives of his disciples is to be mingled with the mass of the world's selfishness and sin until the whole shall be leavened. He who seeks entire seclusion from society puts himself, therefore, wholly out of all relation to the work of God in the world, and refuses to employ the method that God has chosen and consecrated.

But association with men for a benevolent purpose is one thing, and an unrestrained intercourse with the evil of the world is quite another thing. Mr. Edward Denison, a man of wealth and devoted Christian character, made his home in one of the worst districts of London, and spent his life there in trying to lift up the fallen and to befriend the friendless. By such a life as this he showed himself not only a saint but a Christian hero. If he had gone into that neighborhood simply to find companionship, casting himself into the filthy currents of its bad society and drifting with them, he would have speedily sunk down among the dregs of humanity.

This, then, is the other extreme of which I spoke — that of the reckless pleasure-seeker who rushes into all kinds of associations, not with any purpose of reclaiming the vicious with whom he consorts, but simply for the excitements of society. If a man is on fire with a philanthropic purpose, his contact with bad men may not harm him; but if he has no such consuming desire to do men good, if his association with men is only that of companionship, if he does not know that the virtue in him is so positive and vigorous that it will overpower their vice, then he may well pray, "Lead me not into temptation!"

Exposure to these direct assaults of moral evil is indeed far more to be dreaded and far more diligently to be guarded against than exposure to suffering. It is natural and right, as we have seen, to ask the Lord to spare us the bitter anguish of great losses and sore trials, but there is deeper and stronger reason why we should ask him to shield us from the poisoned arrows of vice and sin. There is far greater danger to our characters in the contact with sin than in the endurance of suffering or sorrow.

I wish that I could impress this truth upon the minds of all the boys and girls, of all the young men and maidens, to whom, in any way, these words may come. When you offer the Lord's Prayer, as most of you do, I trust, every day, do not forget to let your desire rest firmly and fervently on this petition. Ask the Lord to keep you away from bad company; from the society of those who are vicious and corrupt and profane; from association with those whose minds are filthy and whose talk is vile; from all communion with evil minds, and, so far as possible, from all knowledge of evil things. People talk about seeing the world, about getting their eyes opened, and all that; but do you see just as much of the good of the world as you can, and just as little of the evil. Get your eyes open as wide as you can to behold the truth of nature and the beauty of the Lord, but shut them tight upon visions of sin and shame. I tell you, young people, that familiarity with evil words and evil ways brings no gain to you, — nothing but loss and sorrow. There is one kind of ignorance you need never blush for, — ignorance of the names, or of the arts, of vice and crime. If your too-knowing associates jeer at you for such verdancy, thank God that you are not proficient in such knowledge. The less you know of the things that you are ashamed to speak of the better for you. If by any possibility you have learned such things, forget them as soon as you can. And always remember, that, except as you seek to overcome evil with good, the safest way is to shun the evil.

Remember, then, all of you, old and young, that this petition we are now studying is like all the rest in this respect, that those who offer it have much to do themselves in answering it. "Faithful prayer," says Mr. Ruskin, "implies always correlative exertion; and no man can ask honestly or hopefully to be delivered from temptation, unless he has himself honestly and firmly determined to do the best he can to keep out of it."

We must not overlook the plural form of this petition. It is not only a personal request, it is an intercessory petition. "Lead *us* not into temptation; deliver *us* from evil." Our thought takes in others besides ourselves; the shelter and deliverance that we implore for ourselves we ask for all our fellow-men. And surely if we ask the Lord to keep our neighbors out of temptation, we shall be careful how we ourselves do anything to place temptation in their way; we shall do all that we wisely can to make the surroundings of their lives helpful, and not corrupting, to their virtue.

Especially full of tender solicitude will this petition be as it falls from the lips of parents. Lead *us*, deliver *us*. The larger desire that takes in all mankind is gathered into a burning ray of intensest yearning as it falls upon the group that kneels around the family altar. Look, Father, upon these before thee; these whom our love encircles; these who in the thoughts of the night, and in the labors of the day, are always with us these with whose welfare all our lives are bound up, — deliver these from the snares of the spoiler; shelter all of us from evil!" Alas, my friends, if we would make our practices march a little more evenly with our prayers! God knows our hearts; he knows how deeply we desire that our children should be kept from temptation; and yet I fear that he often sees us contradicting our prayers by the plans we make for them, or by our weak concessions to harmful social tendencies. "In modern days," says Mr. Ruskin, speaking bitterly, as is his wont, yet with far too much reason in his bitterness, — "in modern days the first aim of all Christian parents is to place their children in circumstances where the temptations (which they are apt to call 'opportunities') may be as great, and as many, as possible; where the sight and the promise of 'all these things' in Satan's gift may be brilliantly near, and where the act of 'falling down to worship me' may be partly concealed by the shelter, and partly excused as involuntary by the pressure, of the concurrent crowd."

Let us heed this sharp rebuke, my friends; and when we pray that our children may not be led into temptation let us do what we can to choose for them a place to live and a manner of life in which they shall be exposed to the least possible temptation. Many a man prays at the family altar " Lead us not into temptation," and then rises from his knees, packs his movables and goes with all his family, where Lot went, straight down to Sodom.

And yet it will not be possible for any of us, young or old, wholly to avoid temptation. Absolute freedom from contact with the evil is no more to be attained than absolute immunity from pain and trouble. Duty will take us often into the presence of temptation; deceitful and alluring forms of vice will appeal to passions that strongly espond and to wills that feebly resist. It is not, then, entire exemption from evil influence that we expect when we pray, but only that so far as is possible without neglect of duty, without withdrawing ourselves from the service of God and humanity, we may be kept from contact with the evil, and that when we do encounter it we may be strong to stand against it; that we may be delivered from its power and dominion. Here, again, comes in that complementary phrase without which this petition would not be perfect: Lead us out of temptation; but, when we must confront it, deliver us from the evil towards which the temptation draws us.

A temptation resisted brings us moral invigoration; if, by the grace of God, we overcome, we are strengthened in the conflict. Nevertheless, our faith and firmness will get all the exercise they need in resisting the temptations that we cannot avoid; it is only when we shield ourselves, so far as we consistently can, from evil influences, that we can honestly ask the Lord to deliver us from the evil that is inevitable.

But what is that word of the sturdy James: "My brethren, count it all joy when ye fall into divers temptations!" Does not that contradict this petition? Oh, no. The "falling into temptation" is not the heedless or the wanton exposure to temptation; his words do not mean that. When, in the course of your daily duty, you find yourselves surrounded with divers temptations, count it joy. Do not run timidly away from duty because temptation is there; do not sit weakly down and deplore the evil. Up and at it! That temptation is the bugle call to the good fight of faith. You were in the path of duty when you encountered this temptation; whenever you are in that path God is always with you; then he is with you now, and by his might you shall overcome. Joy, the joy of the warrior, shall fill your soul as you gird yourself for the battle when victory is sure.

"Blessed are ye when men shall persecute you!" says the Master. What then? Court persecution? Seek martyrdom? So some have argued, but the logic is poor. Hear another word of his that must be coupled with it: "When they persecute you in one city flee to another." You need not go or stay anywhere on purpose to be persecuted; avoid it as far as you can without being false or faithless; but when it comes to you in the paths of duty, then know that the rugged way in which you walk leads up the mount of the Beatitudes.

By the same rule deal with temptation. Do not court it; do not wantonly expose yourself to it; pray to be led away from it; but when it rises up in your way then meet it and fight it like a man, with prayer and thanks to God who giveth us the victory through our Lord Jesus Christ.

When we utter this prayer, then, we cannot help remembering that an absolute and perfect answer to its request is not possible for us in this world. To be shielded wholly from trial, to be defended entirely from temptation, — that cannot be in this world.

While we live here sorrow will abide with us, and sin will compass us round about. And yet I am sure that there will always be in every Christian heart a wish that this prayer might be answered in an absolute sense, and a faith that it will be in God's own time. To each of us whom God is leading a day will come when we shall be led out of and away from all trouble and all temptation, when we shall be delivered at once and forever from all the evil. And although we will not ask for ourselves what our Master would not ask for us, that we may be taken out of the world, yet sometimes in the midst of our conflicts and our cares the thoughts of that deliverance and that rest are very sweet.

But not only in the land immortal do we look to see the complete answering of this prayer. For some of us when we pray "Thy kingdom come!" believe that it is coming; coming to this earth in the fullness of the years; coming with all its light and sweetness, — with all its purity and peace. We believe that a day is coming when the bounty of the earth will fill all its homes with plenty; when work will be every man's highest privilege, and prayer the refreshment and inspiration of every human spirit; when pain shall have lost its sting and the grave its terrors in the brightness of the hope that shines through its narrow portal; when there shall be peace on earth and good-will among men, and none shall hurt or destroy in all God's holy mountain.

May God forgive our faithlessness if our lips ever stammer or our hearts ever falter in lifting up this prayer! We know that the answer will come, is surely coming, —

"FOR THINE IS THE KINGDOM AND THE POWER AND THE GLORY FOREVER!"

www.ingramcontent.com/pod-product-compliance
Lightning Source LLC
Chambersburg PA
CBHW020243170426
43202CB00008B/199